First published in 2001 by

Systems Design Limited
The Publisher of IdN Magazine
Shop C, 5-9 Gresson Street, Wanchai
Hong Kong
Tel (852) 2528 5744
Fax (852) 2529 1296
http://www.idnworld.com

Distributed exclusively in the United States and Europe by
Gingko Press
5768 Paradise Drive, Suite J
Corte Madera, CA 94925
Tel (1) 415 924 9615
Fax (1) 415 924 9608
e-mail: books@gingkopress.com
http://www.gingkopress.com

ISBN 962-85198-9-1

hosted by   organized by

gold sponsors

silver sponsors

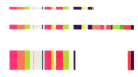

As we step into the 21st century and memories of the 20th begin to recede, we are struck with profound awe as we reminisce over the panorama of events, developments, advancements, movements, moments and forces that shaped the Century and which have all indelibly etched their marks on human civilization. By any account, the 20th century is laden with superlatives; it is unique in the annals of humankind. The potency of political forces that whipped up prejudices and extreme nationalistic fervour that led to the slaughter of millions and brought humanity to the brink of annihilation, later manifest itself in economic forces that wrecked havoc and brought nations to their knees. We witness masses of humanity discarding the yoke of colonialism to form nation states and the ephemeral rise of people's movements toppling repressive regimes overnight like dominoes. The 20th century closed with the amazing phenomenon of the Internet.

What will the Web wrought? Will the next people's "revolution" occur on the Web? The borderless world has become a reality within this so-called virtual world. Its viral fecundity has been amply demonstrated a number of times. It is pervasive and no aspect of human civilisation is unaffected by its tentacular reach. Nevertheless, we are still grappling with the interactivity dimension of the Web. We are still exploring what the Web can be.

Macromedia is in the forefront of this exploration. As a professional Web designer or programmer, you are our partner in this exploration. You are the progenitor of this profound change in human society. You are the exponent of what the Web can be.

IdN and Macromedia have conceived this inaugural WWWhat Awards to recognise and honour the best in the Asia Pacific region. Let me take this opportunity to thank all participants in this contest and to congratulate the winners. I would also like to thank IdN for their meticulous organisation of these Awards and for "capturing" these Awards in print for the benefit of posterity and dissemination to a non-virtual audience. A special vote of thanks must also be extended to our volunteer panel of judges, who must have spent agonising hours of difficult evaluation.

Looking forward to the next exposition of what the Web can be.

Sein Chew
Senior Director, Asia Pacific,
Macromedia

R: 181 | G: 218 | B: 017

004/
FOREWORD

006/ JUDGES

April Greiman // Greimanski Labs studio

Head of Greimanski Labs studio

Recognised as one of America's leading designers and a pioneer of technology with graphic, environmental, motion and interactive formats, April has taught and lectured throughout the US and has participated in museum shows around the globe.

Dave Taylor // The Attik

Managing Director

A studio that really started in an Attic - Yorkshire, England - and whose founders, James Sommerville and Simon Needham, two Batley Art College students, gained their earliest design experience chalking on local walls, but which now boasts offices in London, New York, San Francisco and Sydney and specialises in "telling a story without telling a story".

Greg Rewis // Macromedia

Senior Internet Evangelist

A pioneer of desktop publishing, Rewis now specializes in Dreamweaver, Fireworks and Flash. Drawing upon years of experience and knowledge of Internet issues and technologies to solve sometimes daunting problems, he has consulted on many large web projects with companies such as Fox Sports, Cartoon Networks, American Express, JP Morgan and Disney.

Harry Saddler // MetaDesign
Information and interaction designer, research and commercial development

MetaDesign is a multidisciplinary design firm - founded in 1979 by typographer Erik Spiekermann - with offices in San Francisco and Berlin and a combined staff of more than 200 designers, technologists, planners and implementation specialists. Specializing in corporate identity and systems design, it counts some of Silicon Valley.s biggest hi-tech names among its clients.

Before joining MetaDesign, Harry Sadler researched new document genres with Xerox PARC and designed prototypes of computing systems modeled on human activity with Apple Computer's Advanced Technology Group.

IdN's Creative Team

Needless to say, the region's premier digital-design magazine is itself produced by some of the most creative people in the business, whose challenge is to showcase some of the world's most interesting and innovative designers in an environment conducive to getting their message across to thousands of eager readers.

comment // IdN believes that Macromedia wwwhat? awards is one of the most successful web design contest of the Year 2000. We are excited to see the very encouraging feedback from both the entrants and the voters in the People's choice awards, reaching almost 1,000 entries and more than 140,000 voters participated. Because of the superior quality in many of the entries, we have experienced a hard time yet overwhelmed when selecting the 105 finalists. IdN is looking forward to next time exploration to wwwhat the web can be*.

Joe McCambley // Modem Media
Vice President, Worldwide Creative Director

McCambley is responsible for the creative quality of all of Modem Media work globally. Having overseen the creation of thousands of web initiatives and millions of brand/customer interactions, Joe and his talented team of creative directors may have more insight into what motivates behavior on the web than any team at any interactive agency in the world. A student of consumer behavior and industry trends, he has a special interest in reconciling client goals with the often conflicting goals of consumers.

John Warwicker // Tomato
Co-founder

The London-based design firm Tomato, is famous for its title sequence for the movie *Trainspotting* and its innovative approach to typography. A prolific writer and design "guru", he has contributed to numerous magazines, as well as co-authoring a book (mmm ... skyscraper, i love you). Warwicker was the media architect for Federation Square, Melbourne - new cultural centre.

Jonathan Wan // Sina.com.hk
UI Design Manager

Jonathan Wan started out as a graphic designer for an internet start-up company in Santa Clara, CA in early 1996, designing web sites for clients such as Acer, AT&T, and Charles Schwab, among others. In 1997, he served as an art director at APIdigital.com to set up web design department, and then joined Charles Schwab, as a project manager to implement both Chinese and Spanish web trading sites in San Francisco throughout 1999. Now at Sina.com, Jonathan is an UI design manager to design and develop leading Internet portal in Hong Kong.

comment // "what the web can be* macromedia wwwhat? awards 2000 = B2D2E2S2I2G2N : Business to Design to Education to Synergy to Innovation to Government to Network.

Lynne Spender // AIMIA
Executive Director

Having worked in publishing and the law for several years, Lynne Spender became Executive Director of the Australian Society of Authors in 1992 and remained in that position for 5 years. In 1998 she became Executive Director of the Australian Interactive Multimedia Industry Association, a national industry association for the Australian producers and creators of digital content. She has written several books including "Electronic Rights for Authors".

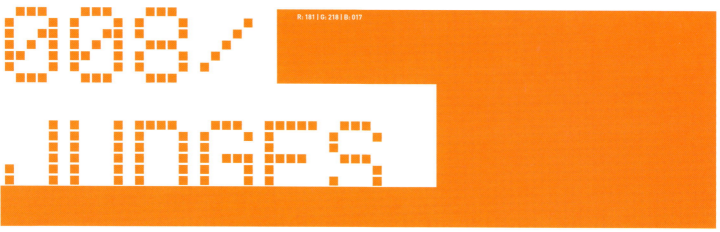

R: 181 | G: 218 | B: 017

008/
JUDGES

Rick Bennett // University of NSW
Lecturer

Englishman Rick, a veteran of the TV commercial and music-video promo worlds, is now an Australian citizen and is currently engaged in significant research into how the advances in digital technology can be best suited to the requirements of contemporary students in relation both to their own needs and those of today's design professions.

comment // The macromedia wwwhat? awards 2000 was a great place for flash designers to come together and view each others work. Whether you are a 'first time tryer' or one of the leading interactive media agencies around, it is vital to see what others are doing with the medium. Of course the same old problems still exist like download time and browser compatibility but events like these awards and the community IdN helped provide go a long way to allowing designers to see how others cope with the restrictions. It is reassuring to view a place where people are pushing the software and not designing to what it seems to allow them to do ... the web is full of spinning fonts, expanding rectangles and dramatic industrial noises, so visiting the wwwhat? awards submissions was a breath of fresh air ...

I was a pleasure to view and judge submissions and I congratulate all who took part and of course to the winners - "way hay!".

Shin Sasaki // Extra Designs
Creative Director

This Japan-based web-design studio does a wide range of graphic work, from printing to the website. Many of its works can be seen on its website www.extra.jp.org. Extra has collaborated with some foreign designers such as Fountain www.fountain.nu and a Danish magazine, Virus.

comment // When I received an email that invited me as on of the judge, I did not know how big the contest could be. Then at the end of 2000, I heard that there was almost 1,000 entries! This is much more than I expected.

This wwwhat? awards 2000 was a good opportunity for me to know what is going on in Asian and Pacific. Because of the language barrier, I had not visited Asian web site often, honestly.

What the web can be anyway?

Simon Waterfall // Deepgroup
Creative Director

Simon co-founded this burgeoning design company with Gary Lockton in 1994 and in 1996 he gained a Masters degree in Industrial Design from the Royal College of Art. Last year he was on the panel of judges for the British Design and Art Direction Awards, the Royal Society of Arts Student Design Awards and the Design Week Awards.

Yat Siu // Outblaze
Chief Executive Officer and Founder

Outblaze is the first company to recognize and anticipate the massive market demand for community-oriented portal services and solutions.

R: 255 | G: 165 | B: 000

ERICSSON
R320sc

LOW BANDWIDTH
窄頻入口
56K, 33.6K, 28K Modem

HIGH BANDWIDTH
寬頻入口
T1, Cabel, ISDN, ADSL

本網站使用了 **Flash 4** 之製作技術，在進入本站之前，請先確定您的瀏覽器是否有此外掛程式，以確保瀏覽最佳效果。

DOWNLOAD NOW!

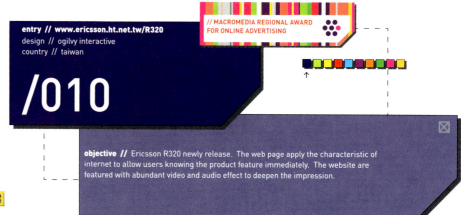

entry // www.ericsson.ht.net.tw/R320
design // ogilvy interactive
country // taiwan

/010

// MACROMEDIA REGIONAL AWARD
FOR ONLINE ADVERTISING

objective // Ericsson R320 newly release. The web page apply the characteristic of internet to allow users knowing the product feature immediately. The website are featured with abundant video and audio effect to deepen the impression.

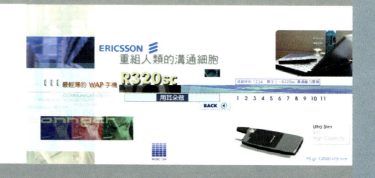

discreet
// DISCREET AWARD

// MACROMEDIA REGIONAL AWARD
FOR BRANDING

objective // This gallery consists of a variety of creative work and ideas that our creative team has contributed. The creative showcase which we have named will be contained exclusively within our EdgeMatrix corporate site. We hope to bring out our collective abilities in EdgeMatrix and to create an awareness of our creativity.

entry // www.edgematrix.com
design // edgematrix pte ltd.
country // singapore

/011

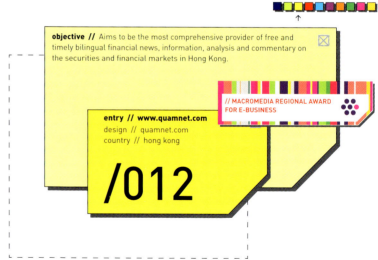

objective // Aims to be the most comprehensive provider of free and timely bilingual financial news, information, analysis and commentary on the securities and financial markets in Hong Kong.

entry // www.quamnet.com
design // quamnet.com
country // hong kong

/012

// MACROMEDIA REGIONAL AWARD FOR E-BUSINESS

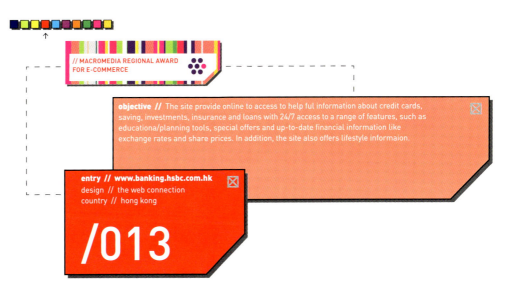

// MACROMEDIA REGIONAL AWARD
FOR E-COMMERCE

objective // The site provide online to access to help ful information about credit cards, saving, investments, insurance and loans with 24/7 access to a range of features, such as educationa/planning tools, special offers and up-to-date financial information like exchange rates and share prices. In addition, the site also offers lifestyle informaion.

entry // www.banking.hsbc.com.hk
design // the web connection
country // hong kong

/013

// MACROMEDIA REGIONAL AWARD
FOR LOWER EDUCATION

entry // www.kidshealthandfitness.com.au
design // deepend sydney
country // australia

/014

objective // The site provides a comprehensive educational resource for teachers and a fun learning environment for children. The brief was to develop an educational resource for Australian teachers to effectively teach children aged 5-12 years the value of a healthy, balanced life and how to achieve it.

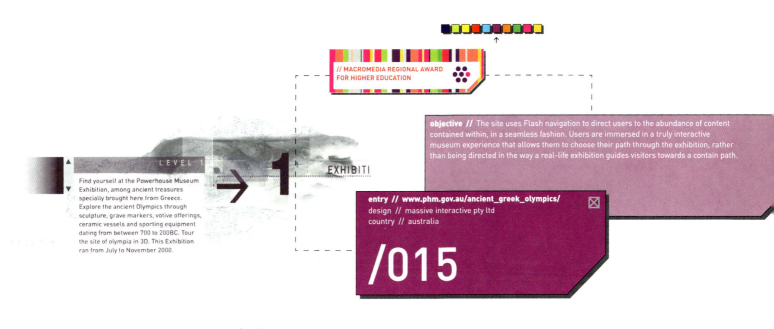

LEVEL 1

→ 1

EXHIBITI

Find yourself at the Powerhouse Museum Exhibition, among ancient treasures specially brought here from Greece. Explore the ancient Olympics through sculpture, grave markers, votive offerings, ceramic vessels and sporting equipment dating from between 700 to 200BC. Tour the site of olympia in 3D. This Exhibition ran from July to November 2000.

// MACROMEDIA REGIONAL AWARD FOR HIGHER EDUCATION

objective // The site uses Flash navigation to direct users to the abundance of content contained within, in a seamless fashion. Users are immersed in a truly interactive museum experience that allows them to choose their path through the exhibition, rather than being directed in the way a real-life exhibition guides visitors towards a contain path.

entry // www.phm.gov.au/ancient_greek_olympics/
design // massive interactive pty ltd
country // australia

/015

1000 YEARS OF THE
OLYMPIC GAMES
TREASURES OF ANCIENT
GREECE

A unit of
An exhibition organised and lent by the
Hellenic Ministry of Culture, Athens
as a contribution to the celebration of the Sydney 2000 Olympic and Paralympic Games.
Developed by the Powerhouse Museum
Privacy Statement

OLYMPIC GAMES
TREASURES OF ANCIENT
GREE

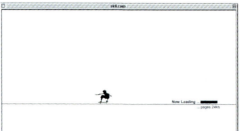

// MACROMEDIA REGIONAL AWARD
FOR ENTERTAINMENT

entry // www-des.tp.edu.sg/course/
d4internet2/project/sk8/index0.htm
design // Leung Pui San
country // singapore

/016

objective // SK8 Tricks is an Infotainment
website that allows users to explore all the
possibilities of the dynamic sport of
skateboarding. It primary objective is to teach
skateboarders new, interesting and creative tricks in
a more engaging manner, while the secondary objective
is gather skateboarding lovers from around the world to share their
experiences and thoughts about the sport.

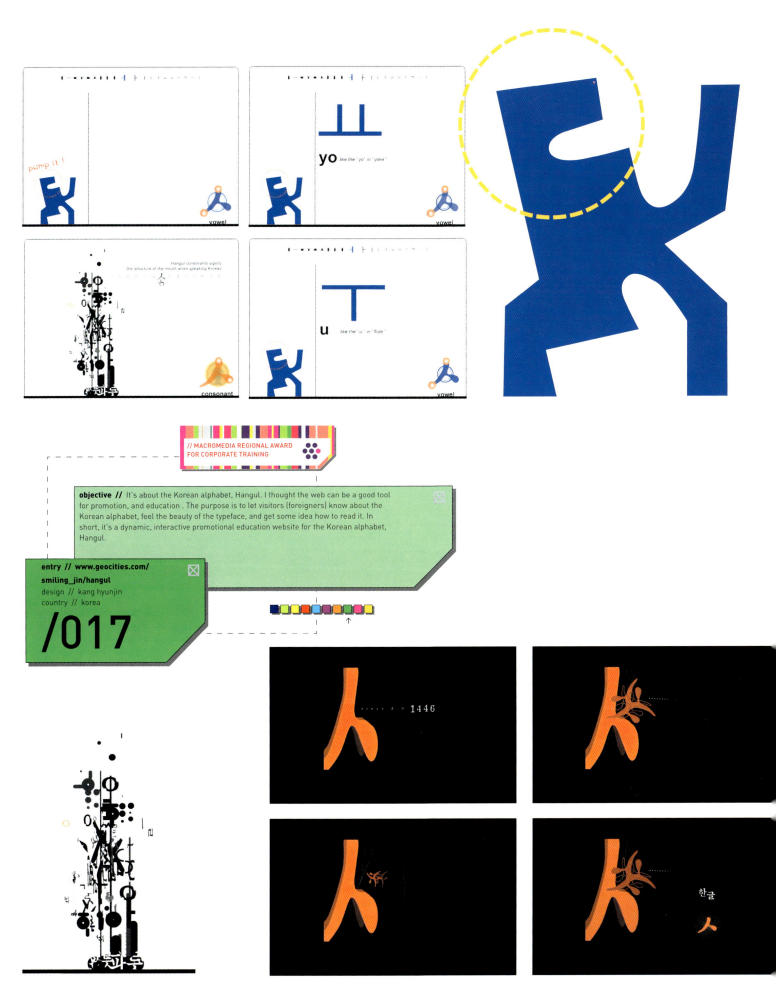

pump it !

yo *like the 'yo' in 'yoke'*

vowel

Hangul consonants signify
the structure of the mouth when speaking Korean

consonant

u *like the 'u' in 'flute'*

vowel

objective // It's about the Korean alphabet, Hangul. I thought the web can be a good tool for promotion, and education . The purpose is to let visitors (foreigners) know about the Korean alphabet, feel the beauty of the typeface, and get some idea how to read it. In short, it's a dynamic, interactive promotional education website for the Korean alphabet, Hangul.

entry // www.geocities.com/
smiling_jin/hangul
design // kang hyunjin
country // korea

/017

since A.D 1446

한글
人

objective // The Visit New South Wales site is designed to provide tourist information on Sydney and New South Wales. The site features access to the large database of operators who provide tourism-related services. The site allows users to search activities, events, accommodation and packages and request a booking.

entry // www.visitnsw.com.au
design // leo burnett
country // australia

/018

// HIGHER EDUCATION

objective // eCourse Kit consists of a complete set of lecture notes, interactive examples, interactive exercises, a glossary, a bibliography (including page references to the course text), a bulletin board, access to an internet newsgroup for the course, and a "chat" service which allows students and instructors to communicate in real-time regardless of their location. The chinese001 is designed for the Cert. level students.
User ID: guest; Password:guest123

entry // 202.85.137.16:8900
design // simple multimedia ltd.
country // hong kong

/020

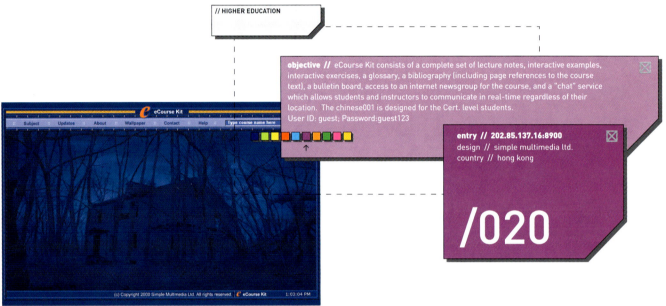

// E-COMMERCE

objective // 4376Zone.com is a vertical portal focusing on dynamic and innovative fashion, jewellery, watches, trendy and upscale collectible goods, lifestyle, communities and e-commerce. As a leading jewellery and fashion accessories e-tailer in Hong Kong, 4376Zone.com was built with the purpose of providing one of the most compelling shopping experience around. With essential functions like real time transaction, product search, auction and games, it also features some ground-breaking elements such as real-time customer service through video conferencing.

entry // www.4376zone.com
design // eureka digital limited
country // hong kong

/021

Name: TheOne
email:
homepage:
comments:

What you mean the guy in atomic attack is the best in Hong Kong? Are you the owner itself? The site is nothing special! Many common designers can do that! I really don't know why you are so amazed...weird. If you really think the site is good, you are a cheap designer. I'm so sorry Hong Kong has you such a so-called "designer"

// E-COMMERCE

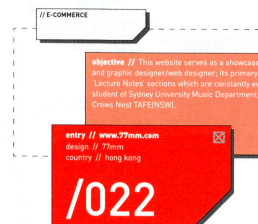

objective // This website serves as a showcase for Beilharz's work as a music composer and graphic designer/web designer; its primary functionality resides in the 'Web tips' and 'Lecture Notes' sections which are constantly evolving areas of information provided to the student of Sydney University Music Department, Sydney Conservatorium of Music and Crows Nest TAFE(NSW).

entry // www.77mm.com
design // 77mm
country // hong kong

/022

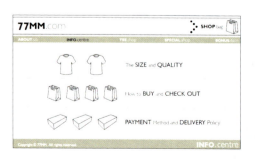

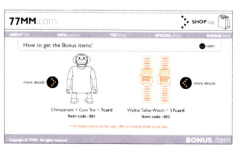

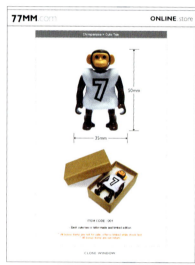

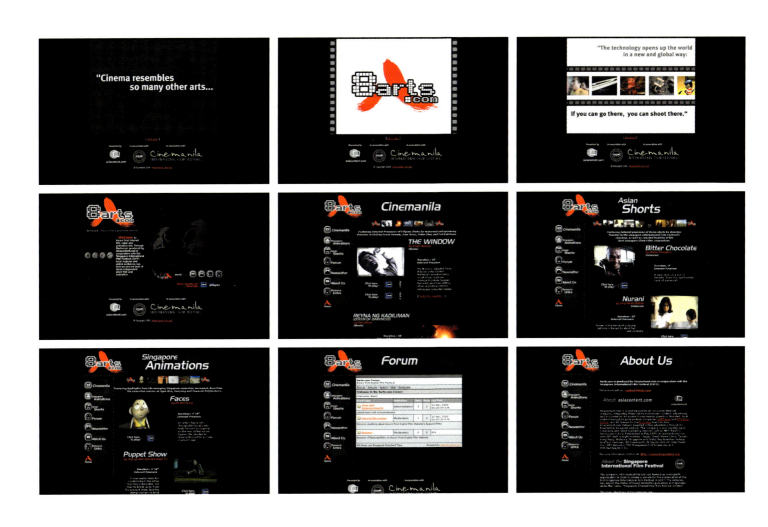

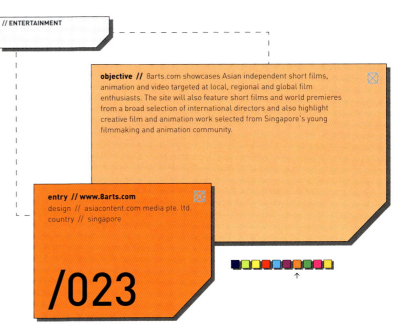

objective // 8arts.com showcases Asian independent short films, animation and video targeted at local, regional and global film enthusiasts. The site will also feature short films and world premieres from a broad selection of international directors and also highlight creative film and animation work selected from Singapore's young filmmaking and animation community.

entry // www.8arts.com
design // asiacontent.com media pte. ltd.
country // singapore

/023

Products & Services
News & Press Kit
Careers With Us
Contact Us

menu::

Regional Offices

// E-BUSINESS

objective // AdSociety — a new broadband advertising, marketing and sales network — that explains the business and gives the impression of a broadband experience over narrowband. The creative concepts for the site were also extended to the offline print advertising campaign. ⊠

entry // www.adsociety.com ⊠
design // lemon(asia) Ltd
country // hong kong

/024

.11 Hey, where's my space?

By Lina Tan

against the grain · issue 11

I hate cellphones - whether small, slim, sleek, black and hip or colourful, chunky and chunky. It is technology at its worst. Why would anyone want to be reached 24 hours a day, seven days a week, 365 days a year? Who is that indispensable?

Why is there this need for constant and instant communication anywhere, and at anytime, during one's waking hours? And what kind of need is this? For hundreds of years, we have all functioned very well in buses, subways, shopping centres, hawker centres, on roads, at public swimming pools, in restaurants, at the mamak stall, in libraries and in cinemas without telephones and without the knowledge or (in)security of being in the mode of instant accessibility.

objective // To showcase Malaysian arts and literature talents to the world.

// ENTERTAINMENT

entry // www.againstthegrain.com
design // against the grain sdn. bhd.
country // malaysia

/025

AGAINST THE GRAIN 11
://SEPTEMBER2000 DRAG DOWN MENU

entertainMENT

MOVIE MARATHON   FACE THE MUSIC   BOOKCASE

ALBUM OF THE MONTH

MARTHA MEET FRANK,   ACOUSTIC ALCHEMY   THE CHILDREN'S
DANIEL AND LAURENCE   The Beautiful Game   ILLUSTRATED
                                           ENCYCLOPEDIA OF HEAVEN

BOSSA NOVA   BB KING & ERIC CLAPTON   HARRY POTTER AND THE
                     Riding With The King   GOBLET OF FIRE

SCARY MOVIE   PAUL SIMON
                     Greatest Hits

AGAINST THE GRAIN 12
://OCTOBER2000 DRAG DOWN MENU

TABLE OF CONTENTS

PRINT THIS PAGE
ADD TO FAVOURITES

AGAINST THE GRAIN 11
://SEPTEMBER2000 DRAG DOWN MENU

TABLE OF CONTENTS

AGAINST THE GRAIN 11
://SEPTEMBER2000 DRAG DOWN MENU

BELIEVE I CAN
The Joys Of Folding Paper Airplanes

I wear pretty thick glasses. If not for that wonderful creation called "high-index glass," I would be looking like a goldfish from hell. Thus, my life's aspiration to take flight didn't quite get off the ground. I never even took those flying lessons that I'd been meaning to. Fear of rejection.

And I'm too chickenshit to go hang-gliding or sky-diving or bungee-jumping.

For example, the Stunt Plane can do loops and will fly back to you if you launch it sideways. Thus, there is no danger of it poking someone's eye out. Or if you're whiling the hours away in your office folding planes instead of finishing up your report, you'll never have to worry about the plane accidentally flying into your boss's room. Then there is the Backwards Plane, which is literally a backwards paper airplane, and which flies in unpredictable patterns no matter how you launch it.

Make no mistake - this is a precise art. The folding has to be very accurate, otherwise the

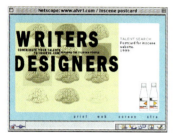

objective // The site serves as a self-promotional portfolio.

// ENTERTAINMENT

entry // www.alvr1.com
design // alviar calarts
country // philippines

/026

Name: LukeHeise 2000
email: jayfunk73@yahoo.com
homepage: http://www.cafe-infinity.com
comments: This site was alright.. Nothing spectacular though. I think the best one we've seen so far is Humpback Oak.. I think most of the best entries would have come in the last 4 or 5 days.

Name: Zone
email: zone@hotmail.com
homepage:
comments: Guys, aren't we missing the point here? 27 minutes to download on a 56kb modem?? Come on.... thats not a site its a lifetime on the Internet. We should be looking at sites that do something to decrease loading times, not the reverse.

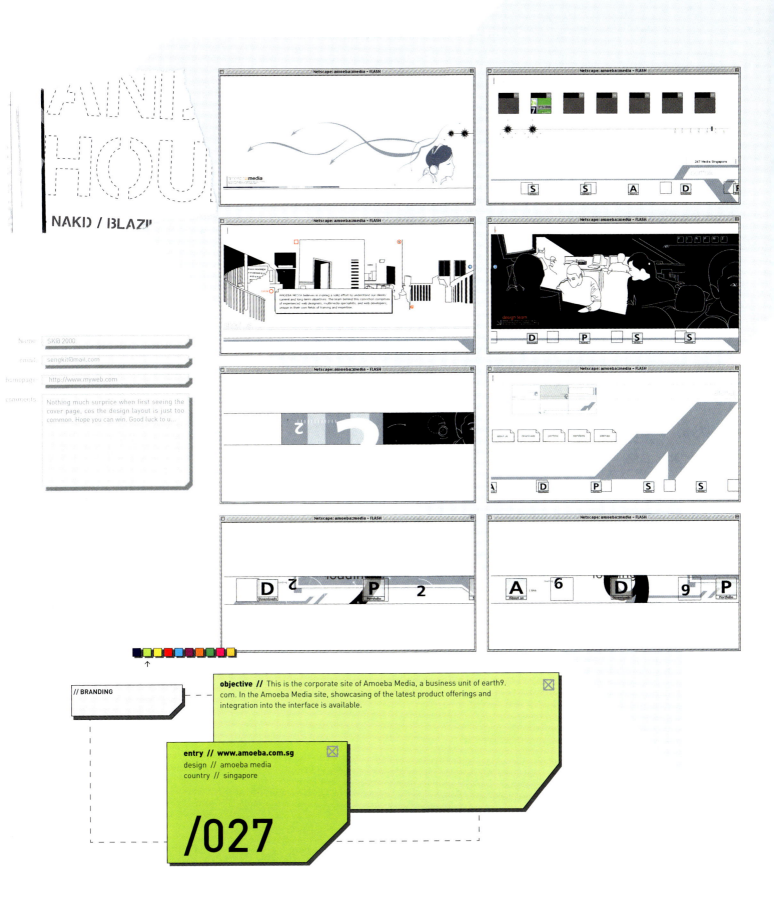

NAKD / BLAZI

// BRANDING

objective // This is the corporate site of Amoeba Media, a business unit of earth9.com. In the Amoeba Media site, showcasing of the latest product offerings and integration into the interface is available.

entry // www.amoeba.com.sg
design // amoeba media
country // singapore

/027

WWW.123KLAN.COM THE DARK SITE OF THE FORCE

123KLAN

SclsTi©

123KINGZ

200% GRAFFITI 50% GRAPHIC DESIGN 20% WEB

HOW TO BUILD YOUR OWN 123KLAN EXIBITION?

1 TAKE OFF ALL THE DIFFERENTS
PRINTED SQUARES FROM THE PACK

2 EACH CANVASES GET A NAME
AND A NUMBER BEHIND IT

EXEMPLE:

KLOR : BLUE MODEL
PART ❶

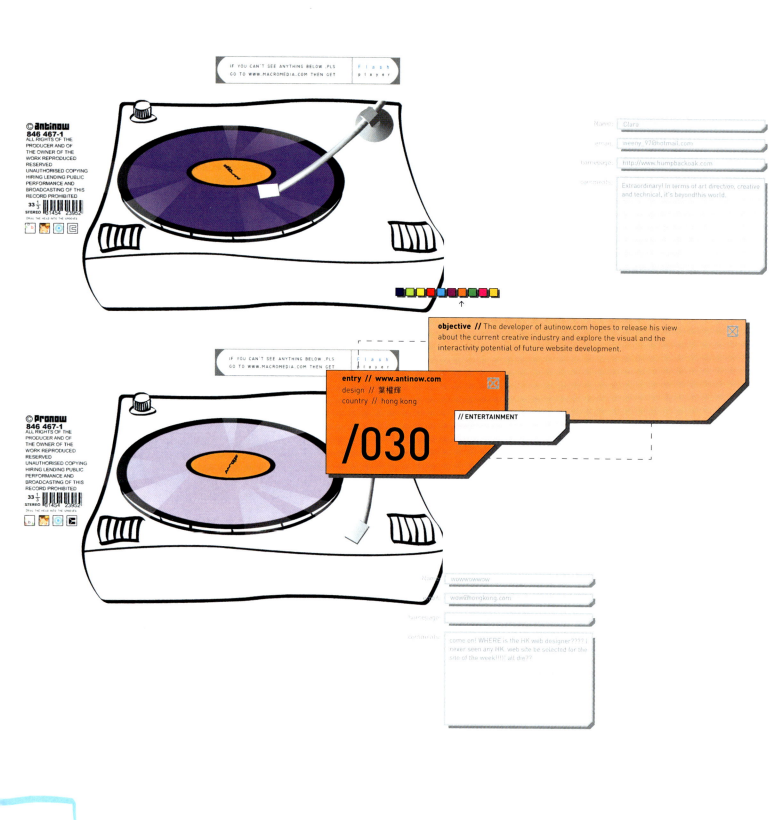

IF YOU CAN`T SEE ANYTHING BELOW .PLS
GO TO WWW.MACROMEDIA.COM THEN GET
Flash player

Name: Clara
email: weeny_97@hotmail.com
homepage: http://www.humpbackoak.com
comments: Extraordinary! In terms of art direction, creative and technical, it's beyond this world.

objective // The developer of autinow.com hopes to release his view about the current creative industry and explore the visual and the interactivity potential of future website development.

entry // www.antinow.com
design // 葉權輝
country // hong kong

// ENTERTAINMENT

/030

Name: wowwowwow
email: wow@hongkong.com
homepage:
comments: come on! WHERE is the HK web designer???? i never seen any HK. web site be selected for the site of the week!!!!! all die??

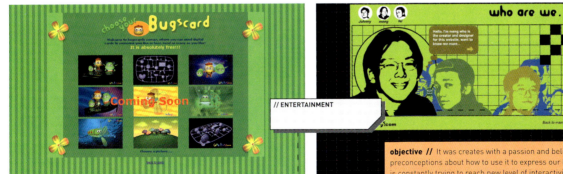

// ENTERTAINMENT

objective // It was creates with a passion and belief that we should abandon our preconceptions about how to use it to express our holistic approach to design. The site is constantly trying to reach new level of interactivity that are driven by the goal of giving the best design solutions — concise and memorable.

entry // www.art-bugs.com
design // pong phui hin
country // malaysia

/031

objective // Atomicattack.com is owned by atomicattack whose vision is about positve, anti-destuctive yet impactful motives through the various guses of design, music, fachion, photography and what you just ignored or threw away. The site request the visitor to leave their inhibition and preconceptions before entering AtomicAttack Inter-World.

entry // www.atomicattack.com
design // calvin ho
country // hong kong

// ENTERTAINMENT

/032

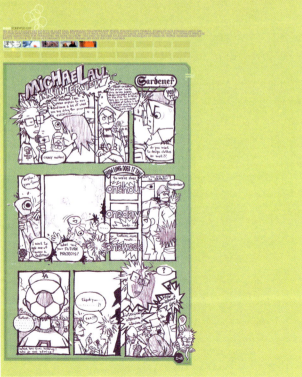

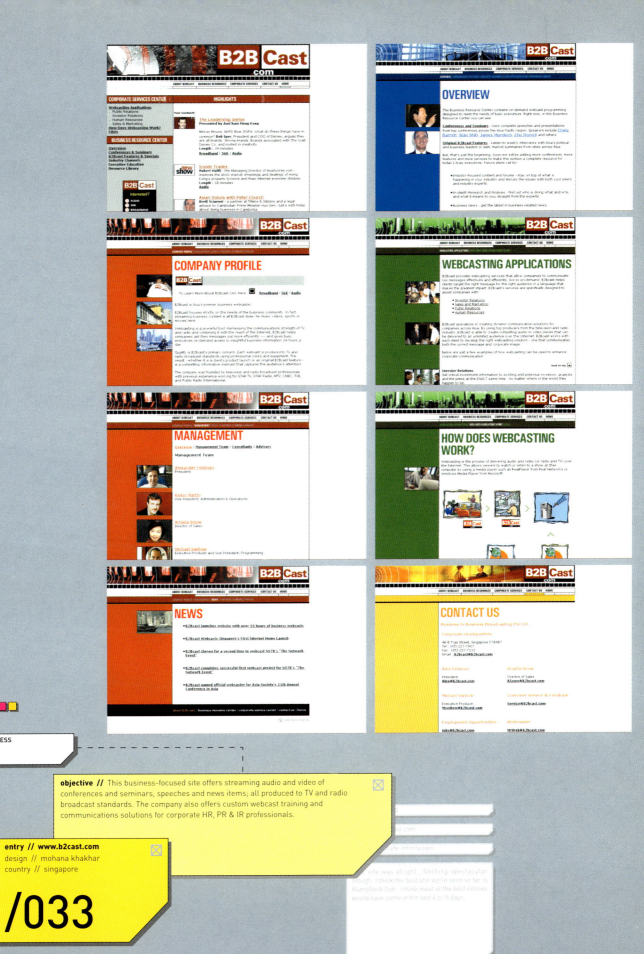

// E-BUSINESS

objective // This business-focused site offers streaming audio and video of conferences and seminars, speeches and news items; all produced to TV and radio broadcast standards. The company also offers custom webcast training and communications solutions for corporate HR, PR & IR professionals.

entry // www.b2cast.com
design // mohana khakhar
country // singapore

/033

objective // An online learning resource under development for the University of Ballarat School of Arts. Distance education students in remote parts of Australia will be able to log in via their web browser to undertake assessable tasks and join local students in tutorial sessions.

entry // www.ballarat.edu.au/arts/online
design // university of ballarat, school of arts
country // australia

/034

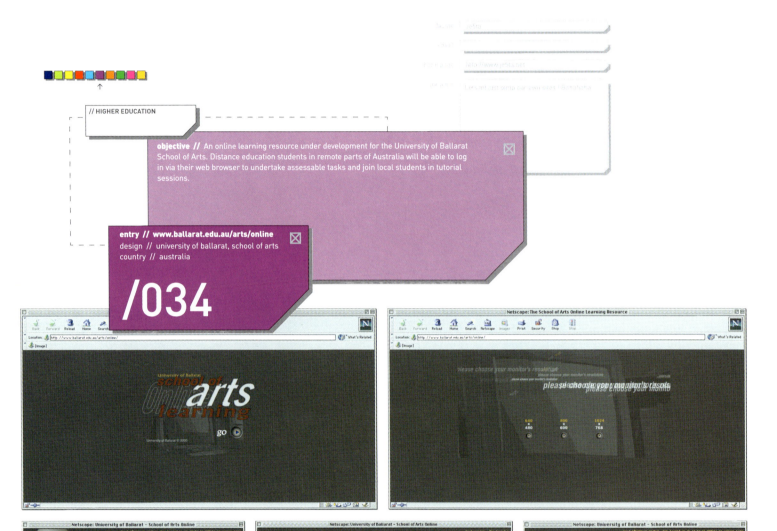

entry // banyantravel.com
design // banyantreeworld.com pte. ltd.
country // singapore

/035

// E-COMMERCE

objective // Banyan Travel brings together an collection of intimate hotels, spa resorts, and unique tours from the most exotic vacation spots around the world.

Name: Magnus

email:

homepage: http://www.merbn.net

comments: Cool site, even though I'm not too found of flash-intros.

Name: Clara

email: weeny_97@hotmail.com

homepage: http://www.humpbackoak.com

comments: Extraordinary! In terms of art direction, creative and technical, it's beyond this world.

entry // www.burkeandwillst.net
design // state library of victoria
country // australia

// GOVERNMENT

/036

objective // Purpose — to create the world's first authoritative website on the explorers Burke and Wills reflecting the depth of the State Library of Victoria's collection.

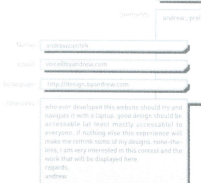

powerfully cold online

verifyPlugins   plugins   enter

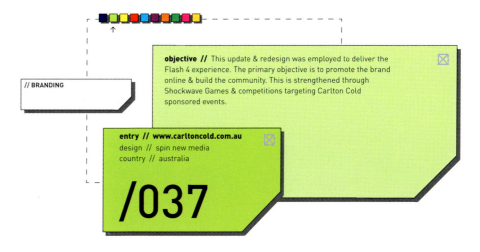

// BRANDING

objective // This update & redesign was employed to deliver the Flash 4 experience. The primary objective is to promote the brand online & build the community. This is strengthened through Shockwave Games & competitions targeting Carlton Cold sponsored events.

entry // www.carltoncold.com.au
design // spin new media
country // australia

/037

orm of varying currents in an electric circuit in order that they may be transmi

entry // www.cathypacific.com
design // the web connection
country // hong kong

// E-COMMERCE

/040

objective // Cathaypacific.com is the officail site Cathay Pacific. The site not only serves as the outlet of coporate news, but also provides on-line booking and some interesting features, such as sending e-cards, downloading wallpaper and screensavers.

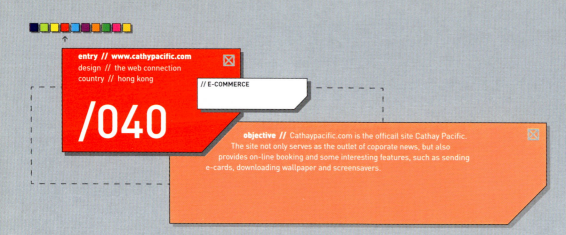

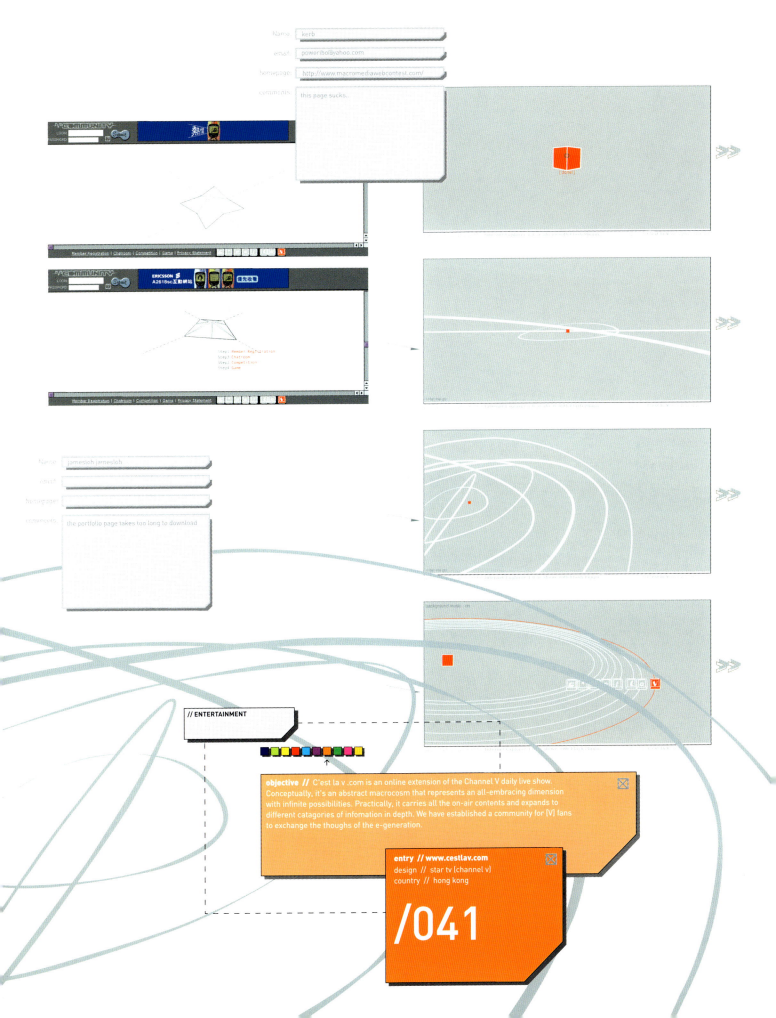

Name: kerb

email: poweribol@yahoo.com

homepage: http://www.macromediawebcontest.com/

comments: this page sucks..

Name: jamesloh jamesloh

comments: the portfolio page takes too long to download

// ENTERTAINMENT

objective // C'est la v .com is an online extension of the Channel V daily live show. Conceptually, it's an abstract macrocosm that represents an all-embracing dimension with infinite possibilities. Practically, it carries all the on-air contents and expands to different catagories of infomation in depth. We have established a community for [V] fans to exchange the thoughs of the e-generation.

entry // www.cestlav.com
design // star tv [channel v]
country // hong kong

/041

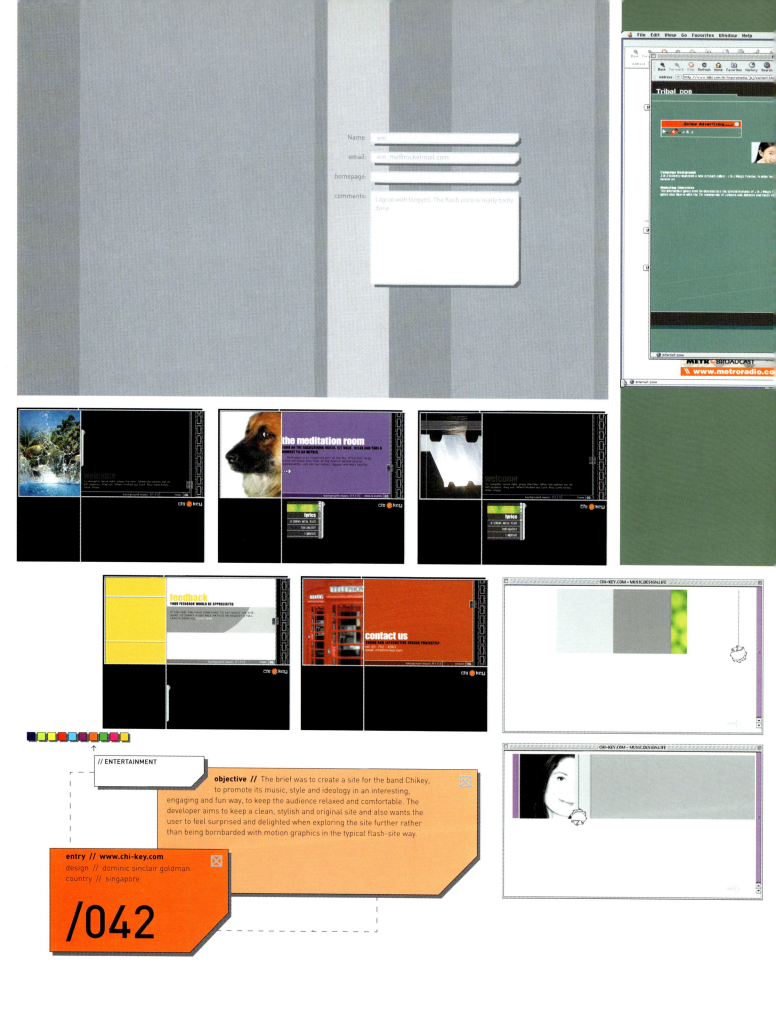

Name: em

email: em_me@rocketmail.com

homepage:

comments: I agree with loopy65. The flash intro is really badly done

the meditation room
TURN ON THE BACKGROUND MUSIC, SIT BACK, RELAX AND TAKE A MOMENT TO GO WITHIN.

welcome

feedback
YOUR FEEDBACK WOULD BE APPRECIATED

contact us
SOUND AND INTERACTIVE DESIGN PROJECTS?

CHI-KEY.COM - MUSIC.DESIGN.LIFE

// ENTERTAINMENT

objective // The brief was to create a site for the band Chikey, to promote its music, style and ideology in an interesting, engaging and fun way, to keep the audience relaxed and comfortable. The developer aims to keep a clean, stylish and original site and also wants the user to feel surprised and delighted when exploring the site further rather than being bornbarded with motion graphics in the typical flash-site way.

entry // www.chi-key.com
design // dominic sinclair goldman
country // singapore

/042

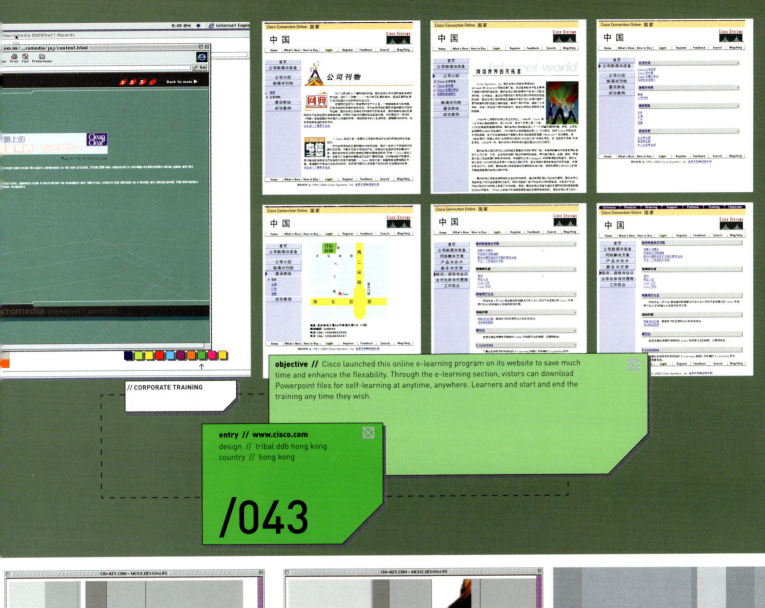

// CORPORATE TRAINING

objective // Cisco launched this online e-learning program on its website to save much time and enhance the flexability. Through the e-learning section, vistors can download Powerpoint files for self-learning at anytime, anywhere. Learners and start and end the training any time they wish.

entry // www.cisco.com
design // tribal ddb hong kong
country // hong kong

/043

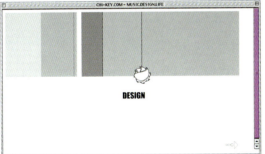

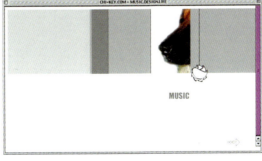

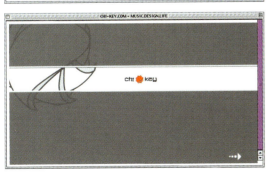

Name   loopy65

email: loopy65.geo@yahoo.com

homepage: http://www.tellyfish.com

comments: Sorry guys but sponge.com has to be everything an ecommerce site (or any site) - should NOT be. Slow to load with a confusing, ugly and annoying interface. i do like the name but in the end did it really prove sponge worthy? Have these people never heard of Boo.com? On the positive side - it's a lovely day outside here in Newcastle. (stretch)
bye.

objective // To provide a fun and interactive site that links the advertising work together with the interactive community aspects of the Internet. The site features two shockwave Director games that link to high-scores pages and provide prizes for winners. Other parts of the site include e-cards, build your own site, and downloads including screen savers built in Director.

entry // www.cocopops.com.au
design // leo burnett
country // australia

/044

Get Ready...

Name | JeSta
email: | JeStai@hotmail.com
homepage:
comments: | i dont see whats so good about it ?! but can u guys check out my site and tell me if i should enter this thing :] ....cause im poor and cant really afford it :[www.jeSta.net thanks guys

objective // The site boasts a dynamic backend allowing weekly & sometimes daily flash updates. Cokebuddy is the target audience's access path to cool deals and great experiences that only Coke can provide. Cokebuddy offers new games every month (Shockwave 7.02) to entertain & entice the user back to the site

// GOVERNMENT

entry // www.cokebuddy.com.au
design // spin new media
country // australia

/045

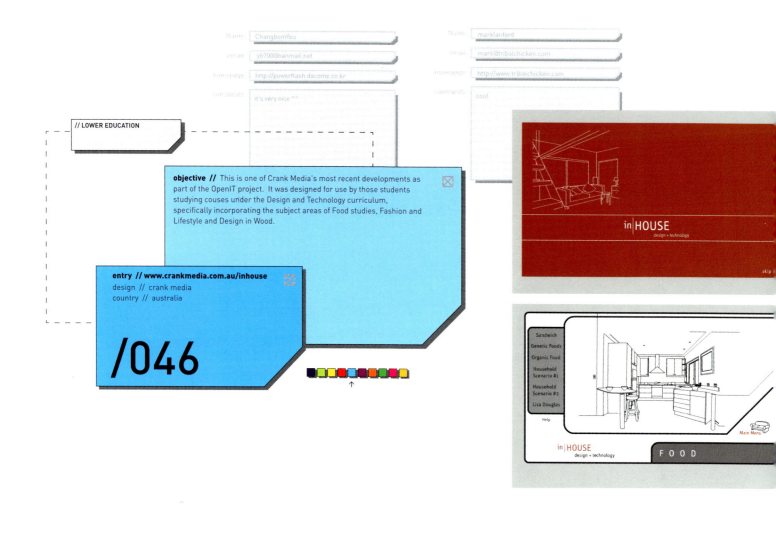

// LOWER EDUCATION

objective // This is one of Crank Media's most recent developments as part of the OpenIT project. It was designed for use by those students studying couses under the Design and Technology curriculum, specifically incorporating the subject areas of Food studies, Fashion and Lifestyle and Design in Wood.

entry // www.crankmedia.com.au/inhouse
design // crank media
country // australia

/046

in|HOUSE
design + technology

skip i

Sandwich
Genetic Foods
Organic Food
Household Scenario #1
Household Scenario #2
Lisa Douglas
Help
Main Menu

in|HOUSE
design + technology

FOOD

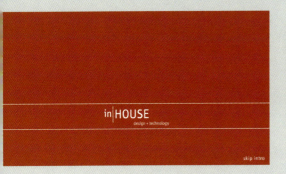
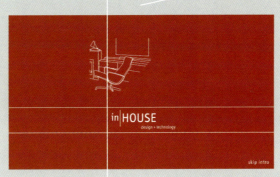
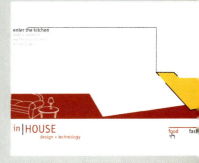

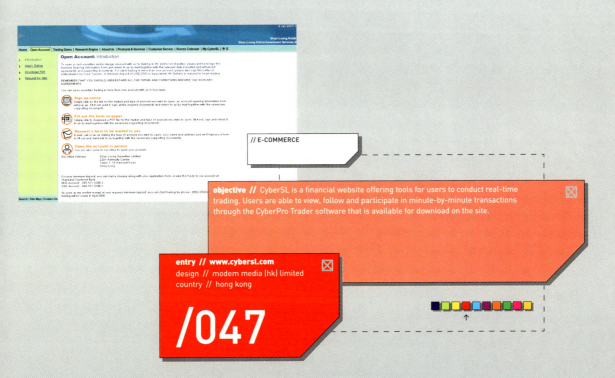

// E-COMMERCE

objective // CyberSL is a financial website offering tools for users to conduct real-time trading. Users are able to view, follow and participate in minute-by-minute transactions through the CyberPro Trader software that is available for download on the site.

entry // www.cybersl.com
design // modem media (hk) limited
country // hong kong

/047

THIS SPREAD POWERED BY:

EPSON Adobe 維他奶

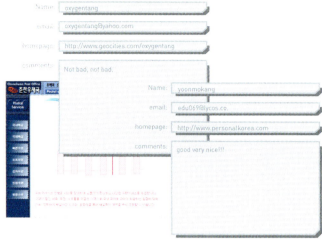

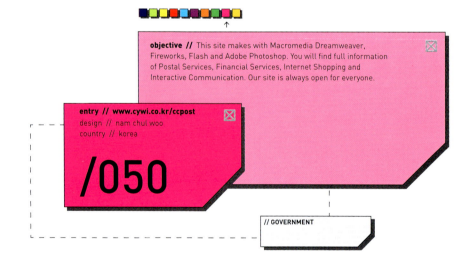

objective // This site makes with Macromedia Dreamweaver, Fireworks, Flash and Adobe Photoshop. You will find full information of Postal Services, Financial Services, Internet Shopping and Interactive Communication. Our site is always open for everyone.

entry // www.cywi.co.kr/ccpost
design // nam chul woo
country // korea

/050

// GOVERNMENT

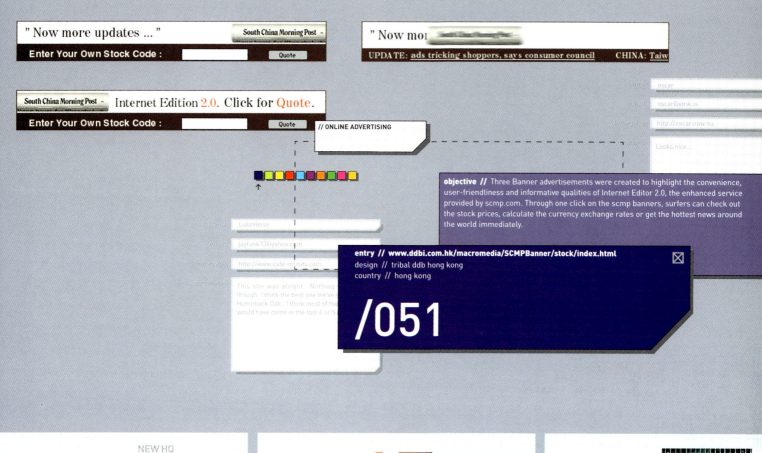

"Now more updates ..." South China Morning Post -

Enter Your Own Stock Code : [ ] Quote

"Now mor[...] UPDATE: ads tricking shoppers, says consumer council CHINA: Taiw

South China Morning Post - Internet Edition 2.0. Click for Quote.

Enter Your Own Stock Code : [ ] Quote

// ONLINE ADVERTISING

objective // Three Banner advertisements were created to highlight the convenience, user-friendliness and informative qualities of Internet Editor 2.0, the enhanced service provided by scmp.com. Through one click on the scmp banners, surfers can check out the stock prices, calculate the currency exchange rates or get the hottest news around the world immediately.

entry // www.ddbi.com.hk/macromedia/SCMPBanner/stock/index.html
design // tribal ddb hong kong
country // hong kong

/051

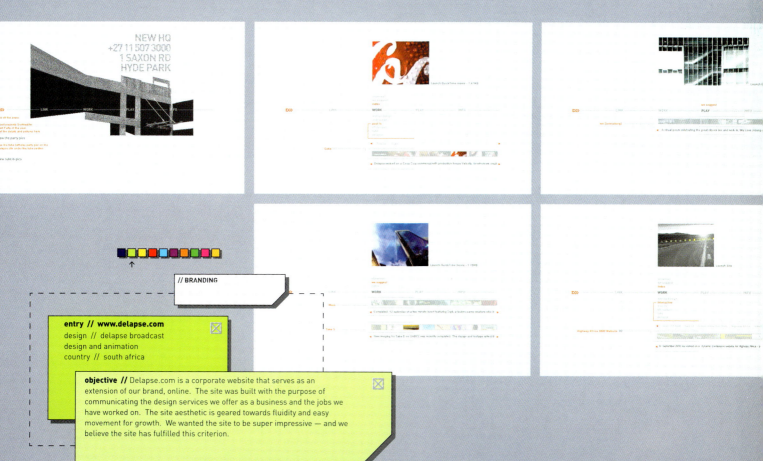

NEW HQ
+27 11 507 3000
1 SAXON RD
HYDE PARK

// BRANDING

entry // www.delapse.com
design // delapse broadcast design and animation
country // south africa

objective // Delapse.com is a corporate website that serves as an extension of our brand, online. The site was built with the purpose of communicating the design services we offer as a business and the jobs we have worked on. The site aesthetic is geared towards fluidity and easy movement for growth. We wanted the site to be super impressive — and we believe the site has fulfilled this criterion.

// ENTERTAINMENT

objective // Freshidentity.com is a one-stop informational website that features articles as well as clothing of the latest fashion trends for the upcoming season. The primary objective of this site is to inform users of the latest fashion news, apparel care and fashion tips.

entry // www-des.tp.edu.sg/course/
d4internet2/project/freshid/html/splash.htm
design // jeannie neo yong ling (temasek polytechnic)
country // singapore

/052

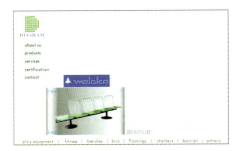

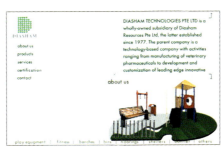

ing the point here ? 27 min-
n a 56kb modem ?? Come
ts a lifetime on the internet.
g at sites that do something
times, not the reverse.

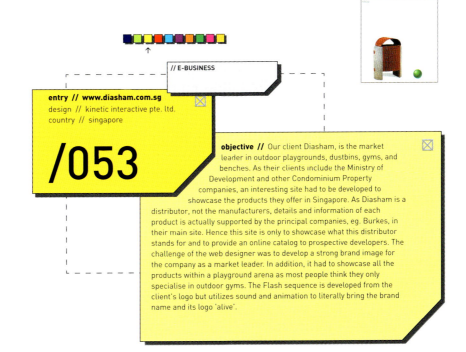

// E-BUSINESS

entry // www.diasham.com.sg
design // kinetic interactive pte. ltd.
country // singapore

/053

objective // Our client Diasham, is the market leader in outdoor playgrounds, dustbins, gyms, and benches. As their clients include the Ministry of Development and other Condominium Property companies, an interesting site had to be developed to showcase the products they offer in Singapore. As Diasham is a distributor, not the manufacturers, details and information of each product is actually supported by the principal companies, eg. Burkes, in their main site. Hence this site is only to showcase what this distributor stands for and to provide an online catalog to prospective developers. The challenge of the web designer was to develop a strong brand image for the company as a market leader. In addition, it had to showcase all the products within a playground arena as most people think they only specialise in outdoor gyms. The Flash sequence is developed from the client's logo but utilizes sound and animation to literally bring the brand name and its logo 'alive'.

Name: Justin
Email: justin_ckt@hotmail.com
Homepage: http://i.am/justin_chan
Comments: I like web design!!!

// BRANDING

objective // This site is for retail chain od stores that sell street ware. The demographic target is for 15-25 year olds with money. The purpose of the site is to advertise the stores and to drive new and existing purchasers back into the stores. To access the members area you must make a purchase in the store. You are then issued a system card which will let you enter the members area. This site is interfaced with the POS system snd updated nightly.

entry // www.eglue.com.au
design // elcom technology pty ltd.
country // australia

/054

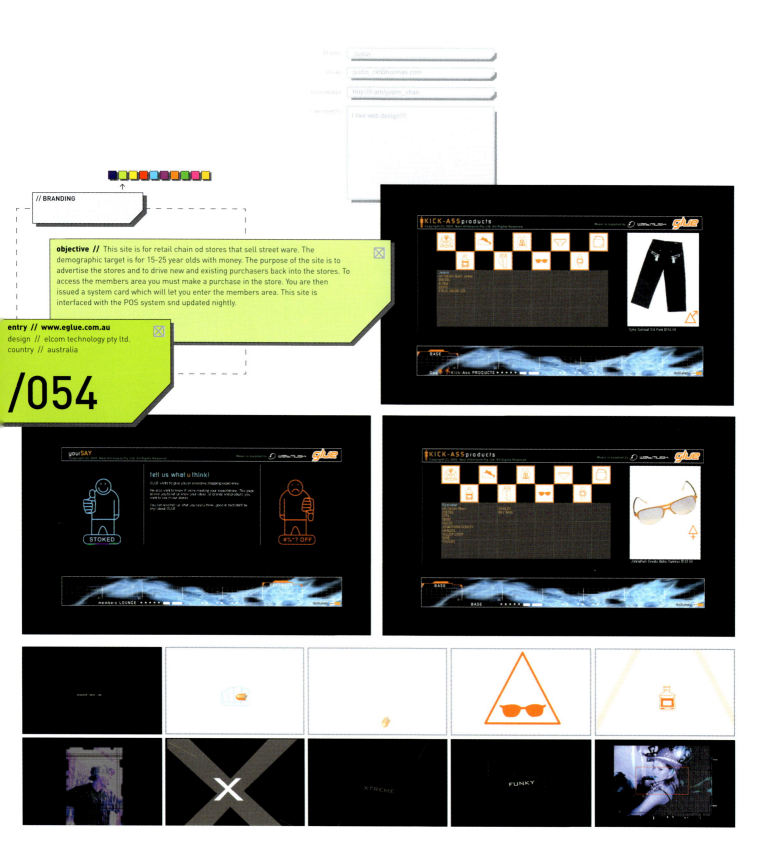

ERICSOART.COM
THE ART OF ERIC SO

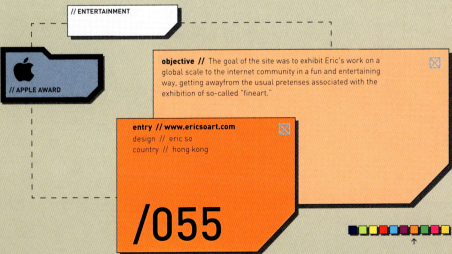

// ENTERTAINMENT

// APPLE AWARD

objective // The goal of the site was to exhibit Eric's work on a global scale to the internet community in a fun and entertaining way, getting away from the usual pretenses associated with the exhibition of so-called "fineart."

entry // www.ericsoart.com
design // eric so
country // hong kong

/055

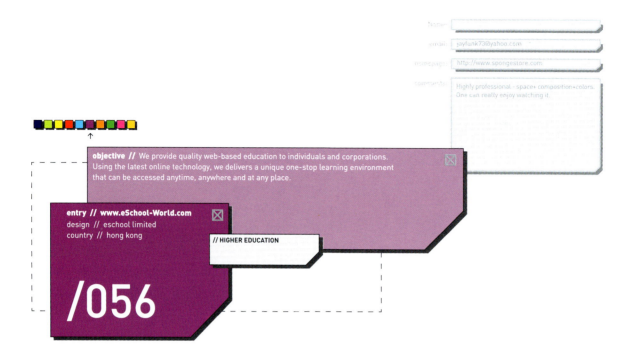

objective // We provide quality web-based education to individuals and corporations. Using the latest online technology, we delivers a unique one-stop learning environment that can be accessed anytime, anywhere and at any place.

entry // www.eSchool-World.com
design // eschool limited
country // hong kong

// HIGHER EDUCATION

/056

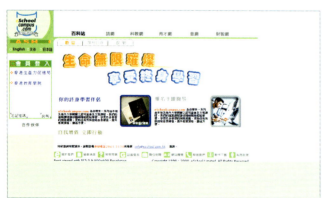

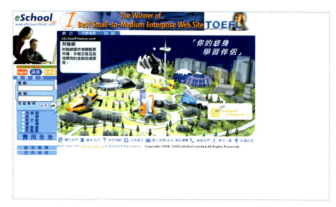

objective // A fun chic cyberspace for users to experience the joy of using Funland's web and Wap services.

entry // www.funland.extra.com.hk
design // media explorer ltd.
country // hong kong

/057

// BRANDING

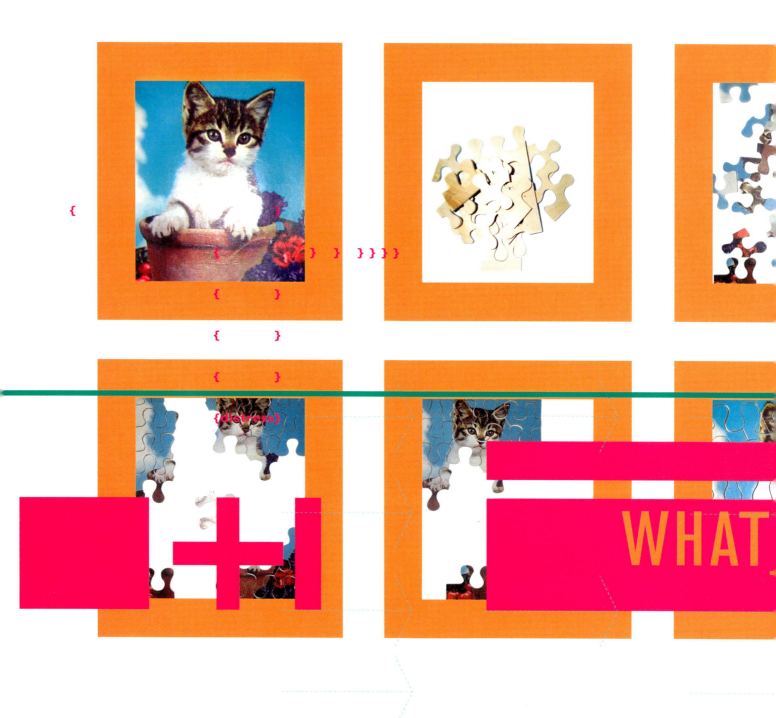

{

}

{   }   }   }   } } } }

{   }

{   }

{   }

{distress}

WHAT

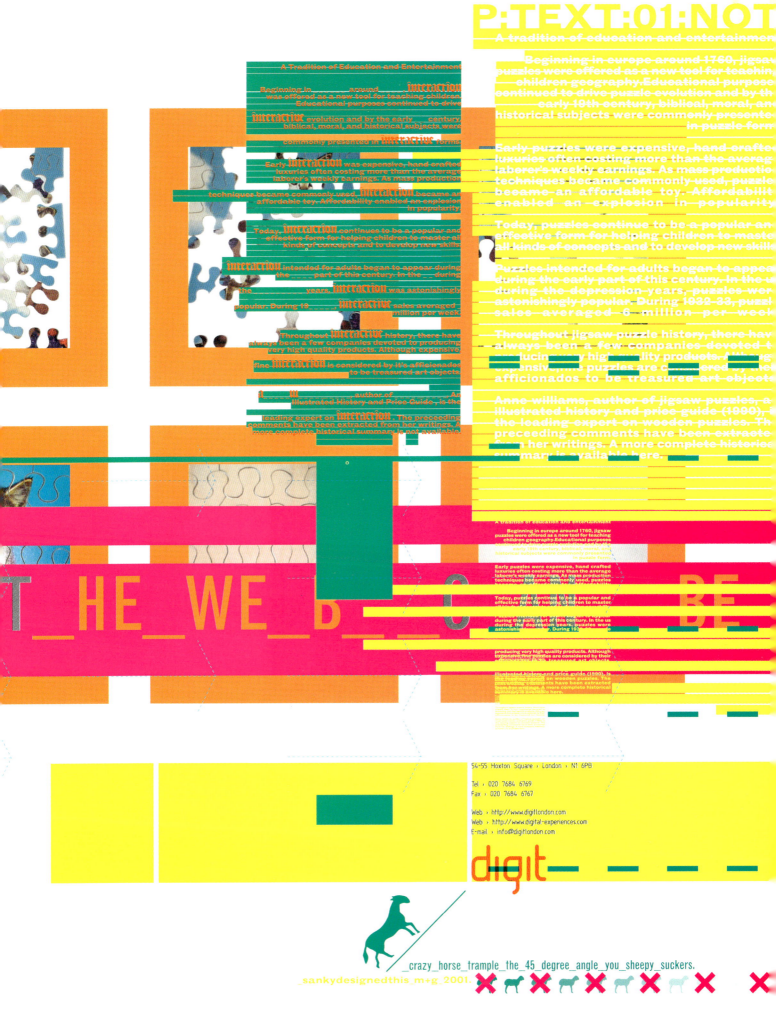

// ONLINE ADVERTISING

objective // Modem Media used e-pass, a promotional incentive for users to register to gain extra points. A three-pronged online marketing assault was used to get the promotional message across.

entry // www.gecapital.com.hk
design // modem media (hk) limited
country // hong kong

/060

Name | Mr T
email: | mrt@t.com
homepage: |
comments: | ooooh....can't believe it......

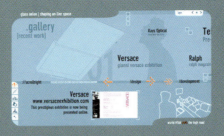

// BRANDING

objective // Funkadelic visual and motion design to enthrall even the most critical eyeballs. ☒

entry // www.glassonion.com.au ☒
design // danin kahn
country // australia

/061

objective // GoChinaGo.com is a multilingual travel destination site (www.gochinago.com), specifically for inbound travel to China. The site supports a full range of online travel agency services and PRC travel-related content for both consumers (B2C) and the travel industry (B2B). GoChinaGo.com is the primary booking channel for itravel.

entry // www.gochinago.com
design // lemon(asia) ltd
country // hong kong

/062

// e-COMMERCE

Name: mindtre
email: iamwinter@hanmail.net
homepage: http://www.flash.nara.to
comments:
made by flash,
i love flash,
flash is my life....
i will welcome, your visit....
vairity flash gallery....
"sadari".....
thank Q~~~

Name: BradleyGreen
email: webmaster@koaladesign.com.
homepage: http://koaladesign.com.au
comments:
Very enjoyable game. Excellent graphics and
Flash interactivity. Well Done.
P.S.
To NigelGreenhalgh, I had a look at your site and
NO you cant do better. I suggest you fix your Java
runtime errors before making statements about
your abilities as a programmer

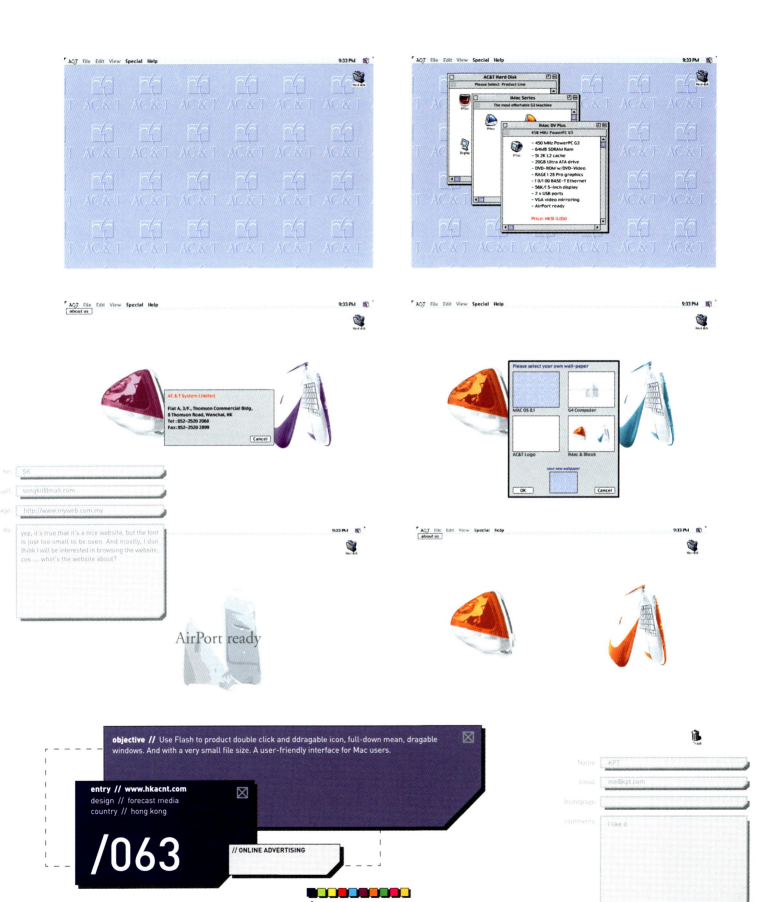

objective // Use Flash to product double click and ddragable icon, full-down mean, dragable windows. And with a very small file size. A user-friendly interface for Mac users.

entry // www.hkacnt.com
design // forecast media
country // hong kong

/063

// ONLINE ADVERTISING

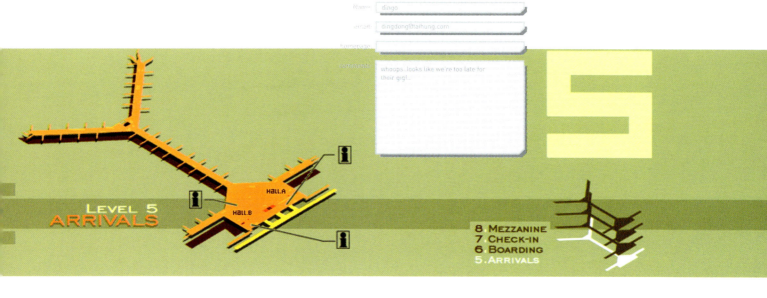

Name: dingo
email: dingdong@taihung.com
homepage:

whoops...looks like we're too late for their gig!..

LEVEL 5
ARRIVALS

Hall.A
Hall.B

8. MEZZANINE
7. CHECK-IN
6. BOARDING
5. ARRIVALS

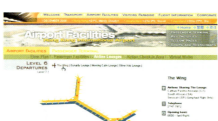

// GOVERNMENT

objective // Hong Kong International Airport is among the busiest airports in the world and firmly cements Hong Kong's position as an aviation hub, hkairport.com lets you leverage its e-portal site, airport transportation, fights, restaurants and shops in the terminal and latest news on-demand. It offers an interactive medium in the form of motion, sound, interactivity and graphics.

entry // www.hkartport.com
design // sasia online (h.k.) ltd.
country // hong kong

/064

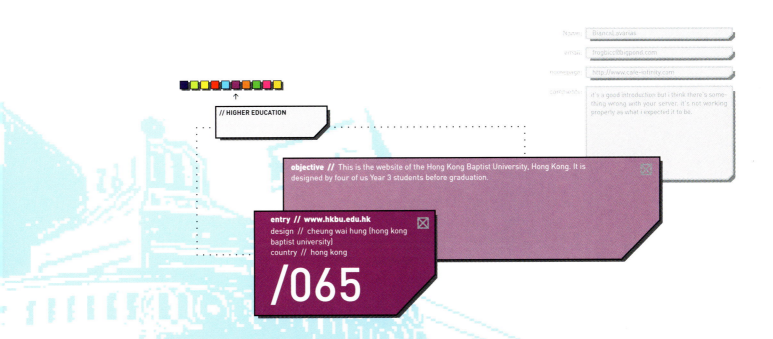

Name: BiancaLavarias

email: frogbicc@bigpond.com

namepage: http://www.cafe-infinity.com

comments: it's a good introduction but i think there's something wrong with your server. it's not working properly as what i expected it to be.

// HIGHER EDUCATION

objective // This is the website of the Hong Kong Baptist University, Hong Kong. It is designed by four of us Year 3 students before graduation.

entry // www.hkbu.edu.hk
design // cheung wai hung (hong kong baptist university)
country // hong kong

/065

objective // HKCEE is the best partner for your studies. Key areas of the HKCEE are pointed out here. The dynamic online exercises with interactive solutions will help you understand the subjects thoroughly.

// LOWER EDUCATION

entry // hkcee.ce21.com
design // chateau consultants co. ltd
country // hong kong

/066

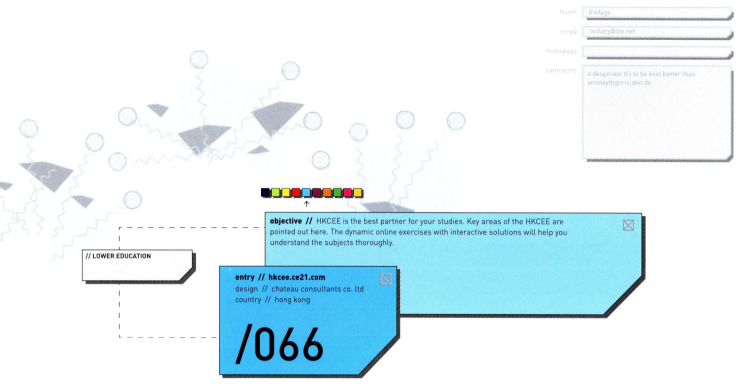

Output:

When there are 5 more workers, the vegetable harvest improves more than 5 times. The productivity of each workers increases.

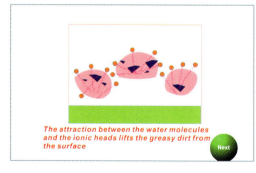

The attraction between the water molecules and the ionic heads lifts the greasy dirt from the surface

Voice of FLYING BirDS...

THE SUN SHiNeS...

Ever since the human race began to walk the earth, we have been dominated by the climate. Our tribal ancestors were constantly on the move, following large mammals on their migratory routes and trying to avoid the extremes of cold, rain, and heat. But in due course they settled, and learned to adapt to the climatic surroundings that ruled them.

Secret of the beasts...

Hunting, habitat loss, and pollution are great factors that hurt the livelihood of many species, but the final push comes from a reduction in some way at the species' ability to adapt.

When an animal has had its home, its food, and its natural

green peace is an experienced independent conservation organization. Protecting forests has always been a priority for green peace. Our ultimate goal is to stop, and eventually reverse the accelerating of our planet's natural environment, and help to build a future in which humans live in harmony with nature... ♥

green peace...

Forest for uFe... ♥

Name: deeps
email: sanghvideepal@hotmail.com
homepage: http://www.sanghvibrothers.com
comments: i think its an attractive clean & impressive corporate site.

// LOWER EDUCATOIN

objective // The site focuses on the forest and talks about how important the message "Forests for life" The design of the site is full of humanity and emotion. In the site. animals and plants are humanized to become characters, just like mankind living on the earth.

entry // homex.coolconnect.com/ member3/anne_ng
design // ng ann nee (the one academy)
country // malaysia

/067

CONNECT

▶ I.N.T.U.I.T.I.V.e. : // TaKING IT BY STORM.

take this media by the hands, lead it to the doorstep of the impossible and cross over into something n

the fusion of functionality and progressive artforms
will thrive in an environment with no boundaries and
infinite speeds of data transfer. the planet will revel
in the welcoming of a new level of consciousness.

this will be the awakening we have been searching for.

the fusion of functionality and progressive artforms
will thrive in an environment with no boundaries and
infinite speeds of data transfer. the planet will revel
in the welcoming of a new level of consciousness.

the enternal state of perpetual communication

①④②⑤⑨⑥⓪

.motivate   .activate   .innovate

4.21 IMG SRC

○○○
what.the.web.can.be
structure.form.detail.canvas.media.streaming.life.knowledge

subjective imagination. ◆◆◆

>>>eternity
IMAGINE THE DATA STREAMS STRETCHING BACK ON THEMSELVES, ARCHING INTO THE UPPER
ATMOSPHERE OF THE UNDERGROUND AND SPLASHING DOWN IN CUBIC EXPLOSIONS ACROSS
THE SPRAWLS OF THE WORLD.

BANDWIDTHFORWARDDONTLOOKBACK.

↖‡↕ 0345 100 100

+   +   +

ERIC JORDAN
aADVANCED STUDIO

objective // Introduced Postpet and its related software. Demonstrations of constructing self-made icon with full illustration and also list of recommended sites is available.

// HIGHER EDUCATION

entry // home.pchome.com.tw/
computer/box715
design // 張文蓓
country // taiwan

/070

Name: GEne

email: savage@pacific.net.sg

homepage:

comments: wellblowmedownandcallmeasian dude, did you even look at their DHTML site? you were obviously too busy criticizing the site to even see the pure genius of it. Go back and take a look you norom.

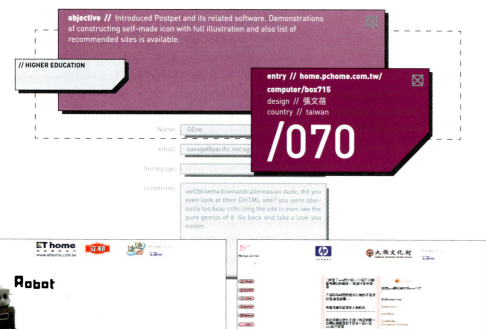

// HIGHER EDUCATION

objective // Its objective is to provide general information about the Fine Art
Department of the Chinese University of Hong Kong.

entry // home.ust.hk/~im_lwxaa/cufinearts/index.htm
design // ko siu hong
country // hong kong

/071

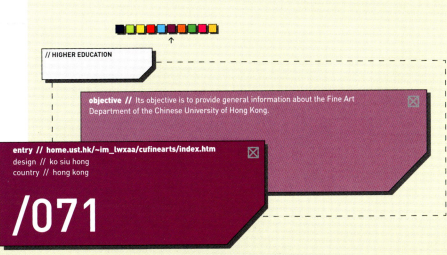

objective // To provide the most comprehensive property and household-related information and services to facilitate our clients in searching for and building their ideal homes.

entry // www.house18.com
design // informasia holding limited
country // hong kong

/072

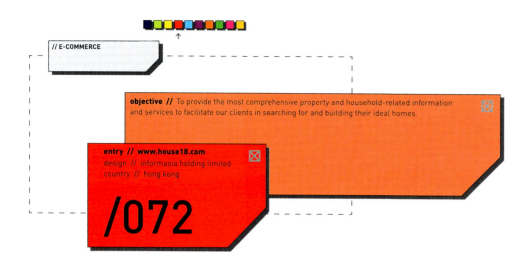

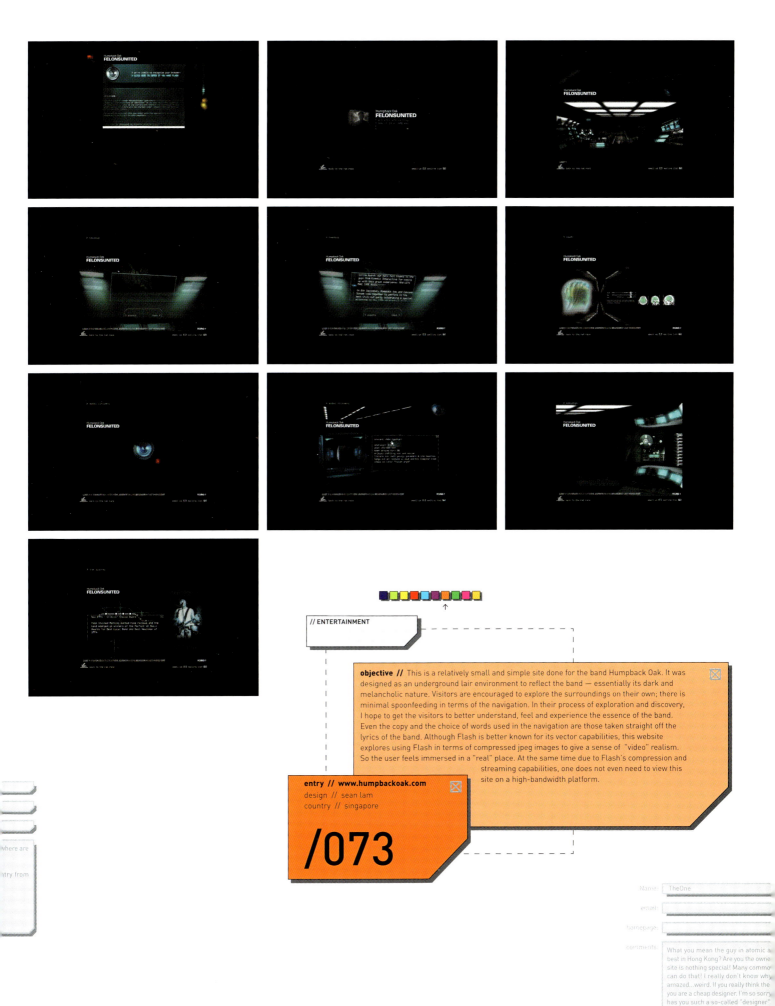

where are

ntry from

// ENTERTAINMENT

objective // This is a relatively small and simple site done for the band Humpback Oak. It was designed as an underground lair environment to reflect the band — essentially its dark and melancholic nature. Visitors are encouraged to explore the surroundings on their own; there is minimal spoonfeeding in terms of the navigation. In their process of exploration and discovery, I hope to get the visitors to better understand, feel and experience the essence of the band. Even the copy and the choice of words used in the navigation are those taken straight off the lyrics of the band. Although Flash is better known for its vector capabilities, this website explores using Flash in terms of compressed jpeg images to give a sense of "video" realism. So the user feels immersed in a "real" place. At the same time due to Flash's compression and streaming capabilities, one does not even need to view this site on a high-bandwidth platform.

entry // www.humpbackoak.com
design // sean lam
country // singapore

/073

Name: TheOne

email:

homepage:

comments: What you mean the guy in atomic a best in Hong Kong? Are you the owne site is nothing special! Many commo can do that! I really don't know why amazed...weird. If you really think the you are a cheap designer. I'm so sorry has you such a so-called "designer"

objective // Hungerford Hill's origins are in the Hunter Valley and it is here — in the old church on McDonald's Road, Pokolbin — that we have located our 'Cellar Door', even if our philosophy now embraces wines made from grpes grown anywhere in NSW. We invite you to visit us and try our range of contemporary NSW wines.

entry // www.hungerfordhill.com
design // spike cyberworks
country // australia

/074

iota

rosekitchen@sinamail.com

http://rosekitchen.com

I saw many good design ideas here.
:] That's very well.

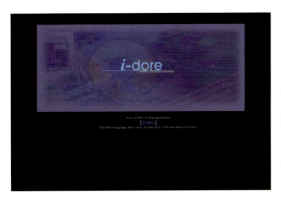

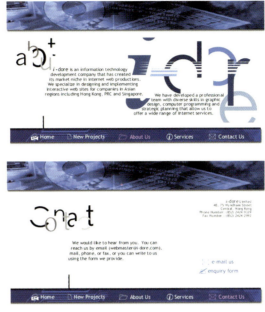

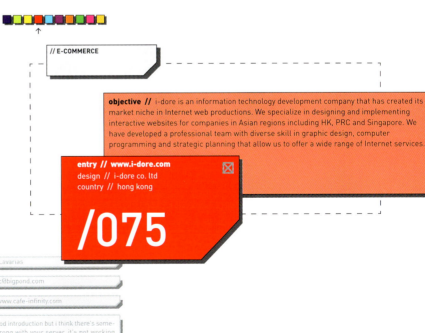

// E-COMMERCE

objective // i-dore is an information technology development company that has created its market niche in Internet web productions. We specialize in designing and implementing interactive websites for companies in Asian regions including HK, PRC and Singapore. We have developed a professional team with diverse skill in graphic design, computer programming and strategic planning that allow us to offer a wide range of Internet services.

entry // www.i-dore.com
design // i-dore co. ltd
country // hong kong

/075

Name: BiancaLavarias

email: frogbicc@bigpond.com

homepage: http://www.cafe-infinity.com

comments: it's a good introduction but i think there's something wrong with your server. it's not working properly as what i expected it to be.

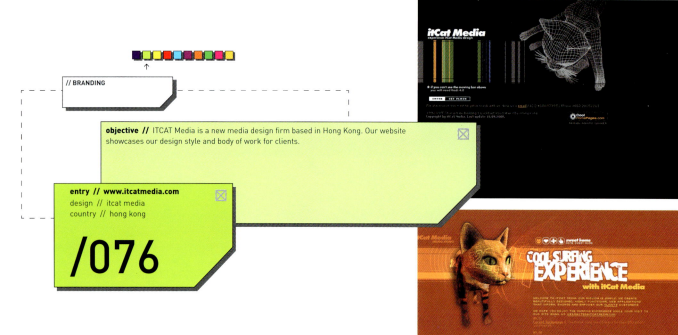

■■■■■■■■■■
↑

// BRANDING

objective // ITCAT Media is a new media design firm based in Hong Kong. Our website showcases our design style and body of work for clients. ⊠

entry // www.itcatmedia.com ⊠
design // itcat media
country // hong kong

/076

en

enc@cyberway.com

game didn't start, wonder what ha
tong to load, I even had time to paint my nails.
ed is a big selling point. No client wo
want a site that takes so long to lo
ect, I think the site has failed terr
s...

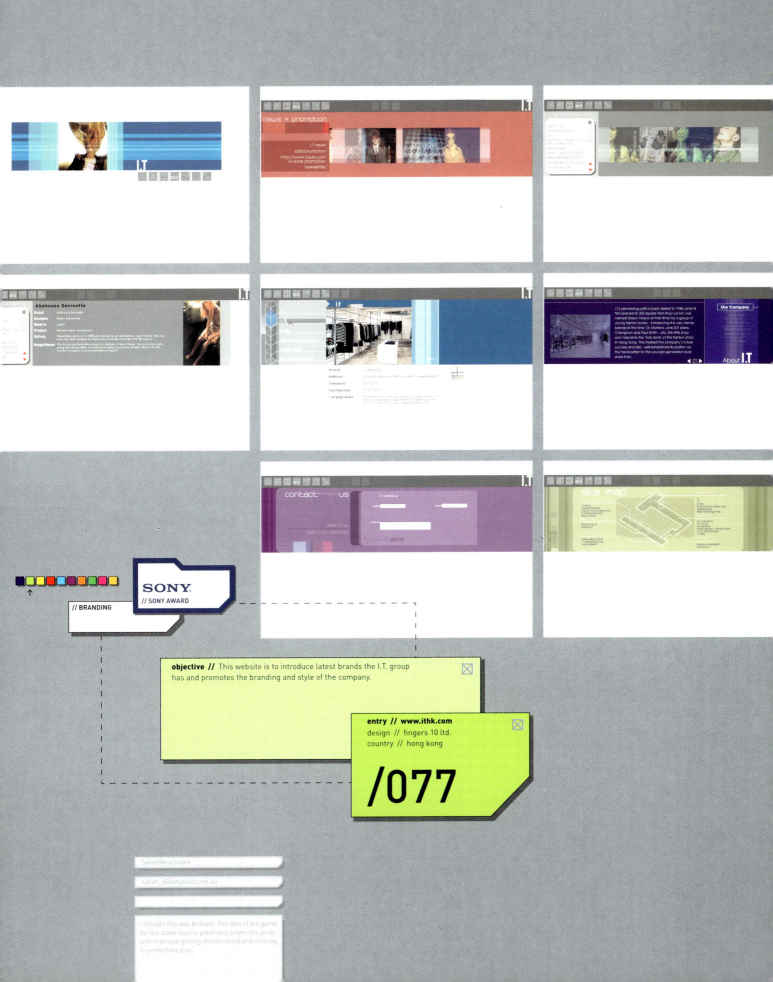

// BRANDING

SONY
// SONY AWARD

objective // This website is to introduce latest brands the I.T. group
has and promotes the branding and style of the company.

entry // www.ithk.com
design // fingers 10 ltd.
country // hong kong

/077

SarahVerschoore

sarah_v@optusnet.com.au

I thought this was brilliant. The idea of the game
for the down load is great and solves the prob-
lem of people getting disinterested and clicking
to something else.

// PEOPLE CHOICE AWARD

objective // iYellowbus.com is the first major children's portal website in the Greater China region. Featuring the popular Hong Kong comic characters "McMug", "McDull", and their family, iYellowbus.com targets to become "the first website in their life" for children and acts as a place for parents and teachers to interact with them. To arouse children's interests, best-of-breed multimedia contents such as animations and interactive games are used heavily throughout the website.

entry // www.iyellowbus.com
design // netalone.com limited
country // hong kong

/080

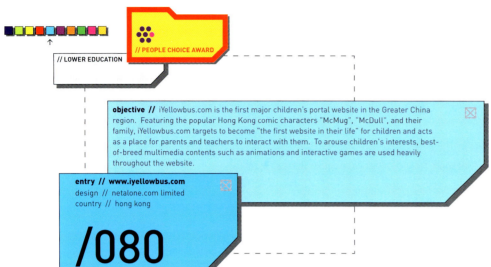

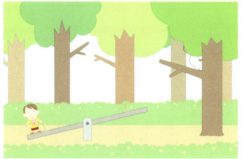

// BRANDING

objective // izzue.com is the leading fashion portal in Hong Kong. With content focus
on fashion and lifestyle issues, it features over 100 brands and designers. E-commerce
is also available for members to shop for casual clothes and lifestyle products.

entry // www.izzue.com
design // izzue.com (hong kong) ltd.
country // hong kong

/081

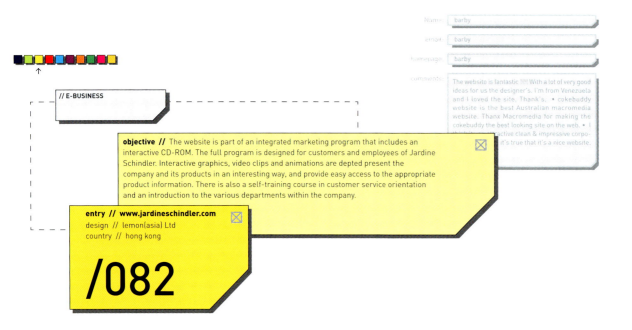

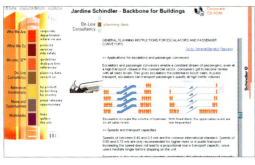

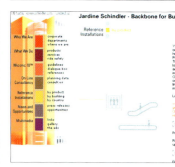

// E-BUSINESS

objective // The website is part of an integrated marketing program that includes an interactive CD-ROM. The full program is designed for customers and employees of Jardine Schindler. Interactive graphics, video clips and animations are depted present the company and its products in an interesting way, and provide easy access to the appropriate product information. There is also a self-training course in customer service orientation and an introduction to the various departments within the company.

entry // www.jardineschindler.com
design // lemon(asia) Ltd
country // hong kong

/082

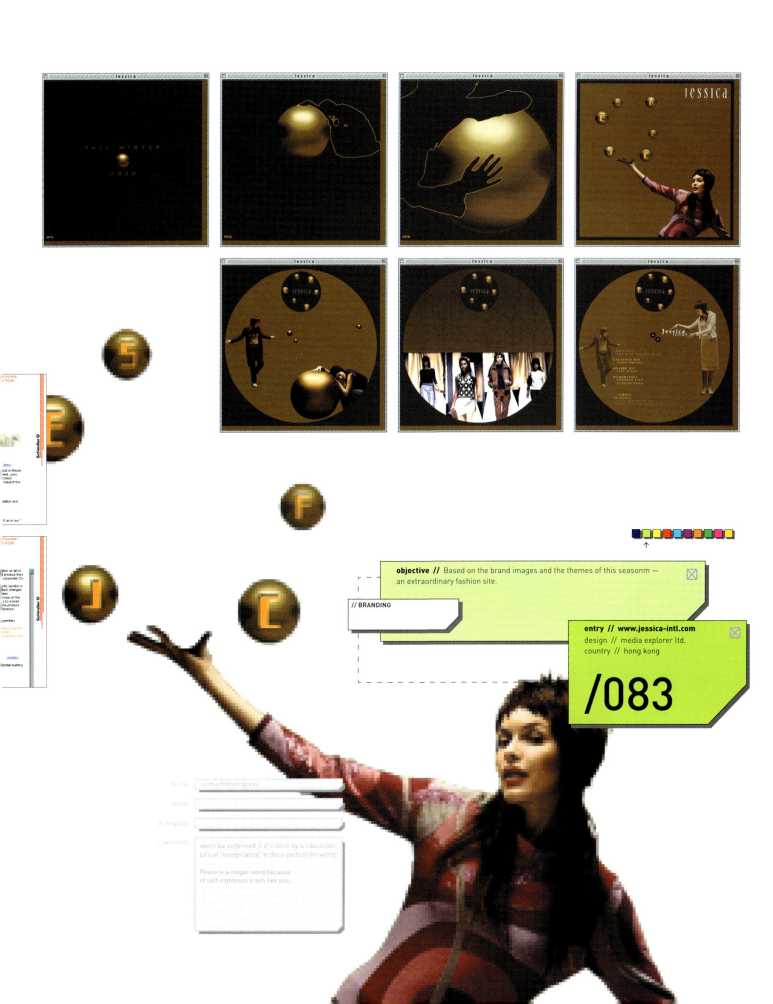

objective // Based on the brand images and the themes of this seasonm —
an extraordinary fashion site.

// BRANDING

entry // www.jessica-intl.com
design // media explorer ltd.
country // hong kong

/083

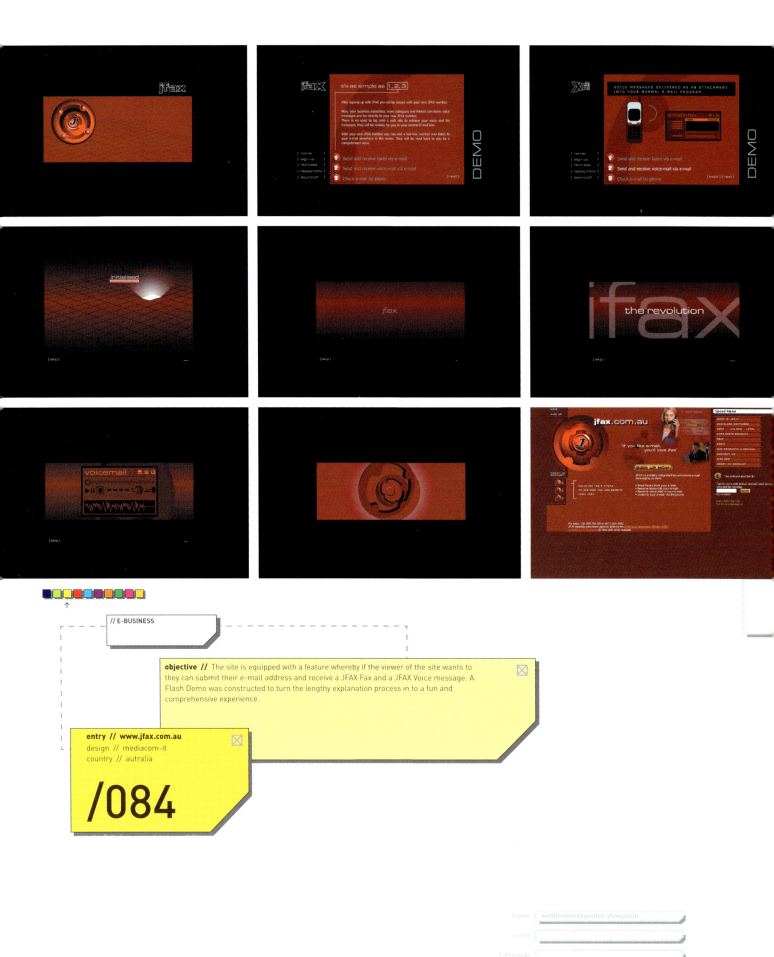

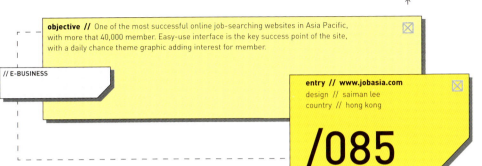

objective // One of the most successful online job-searching websites in Asia Pacific, with more that 40,000 member. Easy-use interface is the key success point of the site, with a daily chance theme graphic adding interest for member.

// E-BUSINESS

entry // www.jobasia.com
design // saiman lee
country // hong kong

/085

Name: JULIETAVINCENT

email: juvincent@terra.com

homepage:

comments: The website is fantastic !!!! With a lot of very good ideas for us the designer's. I'm from Venezuela and I loved the site. Thank's.

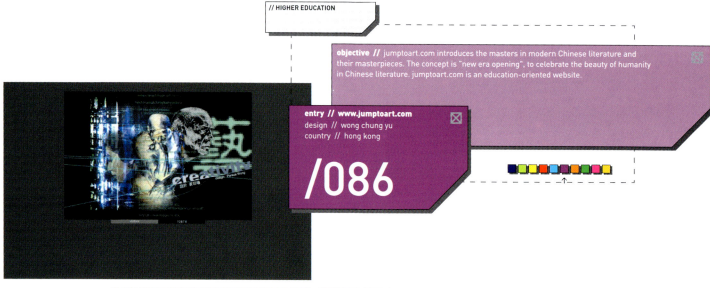

objective // jumptoart.com introduces the masters in modern Chinese literature and their masterpieces. The concept is "new era opening", to celebrate the beauty of humanity in Chinese literature. jumptoart.com is an education-oriented website.

entry // www.jumptoart.com
design // wong chung yu
country // hong kong

/086

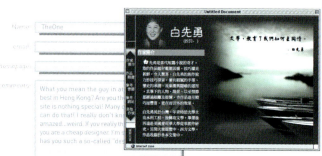

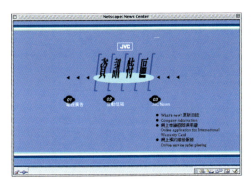

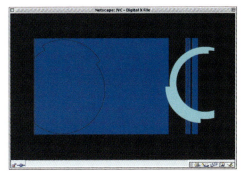

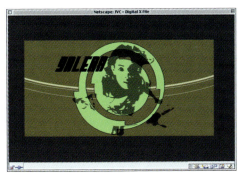

objective // An Internet channel to communicate with JVC consumers targeted at Hong Kong GenXers for exclusively sourced consumer electronics products.

// E-COMMERCE

entry // www.jvc.com.hk
design // lemon(asia) Ltd
country // hong kong

/087

Name: ellen
email: ellenc@cyberway.com
homepage:
comments: my game didn't start, wonder wh
Too long to load, I even had time to
Speed is a big selling point. No o
will want a site that takes so long
aspect, I think the site has failed
guys...

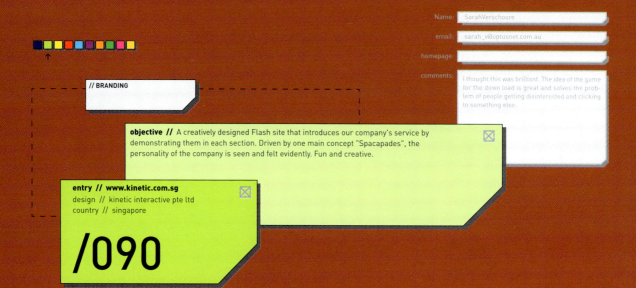

// BRANDING

objective // A creatively designed Flash site that introduces our company's service by demonstrating them in each section. Driven by one main concept "Spacapades", the personality of the company is seen and felt evidently. Fun and creative.

entry // www.kinetic.com.sg
design // kinetic interactive pte ltd
country // singapore

/090

objective // Kungfu Boy game is a multiuser online game. Recruit a Kungfu Boy, train him, and allow him to fight against other fighters all over the world. Beware, because this game is highly addictive. Play Kungfu boy game on the move using a mobile phone too!

entry // www.kungfuboy.com
design // davidcan.com pte ltd
country // singapore

/091

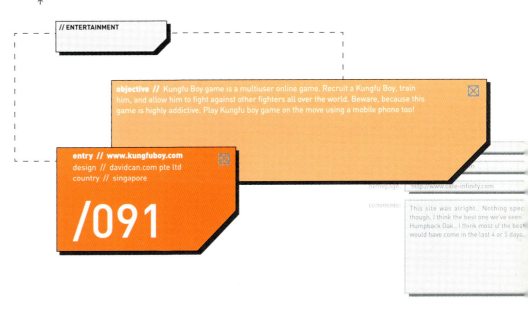

homepage: http://www.cafe-infinity.com

comments: This site was alright... Nothing spec though. I think the best one we've seen Humpback Oak... I think most of the best would have come in the last 4 or 5 days.

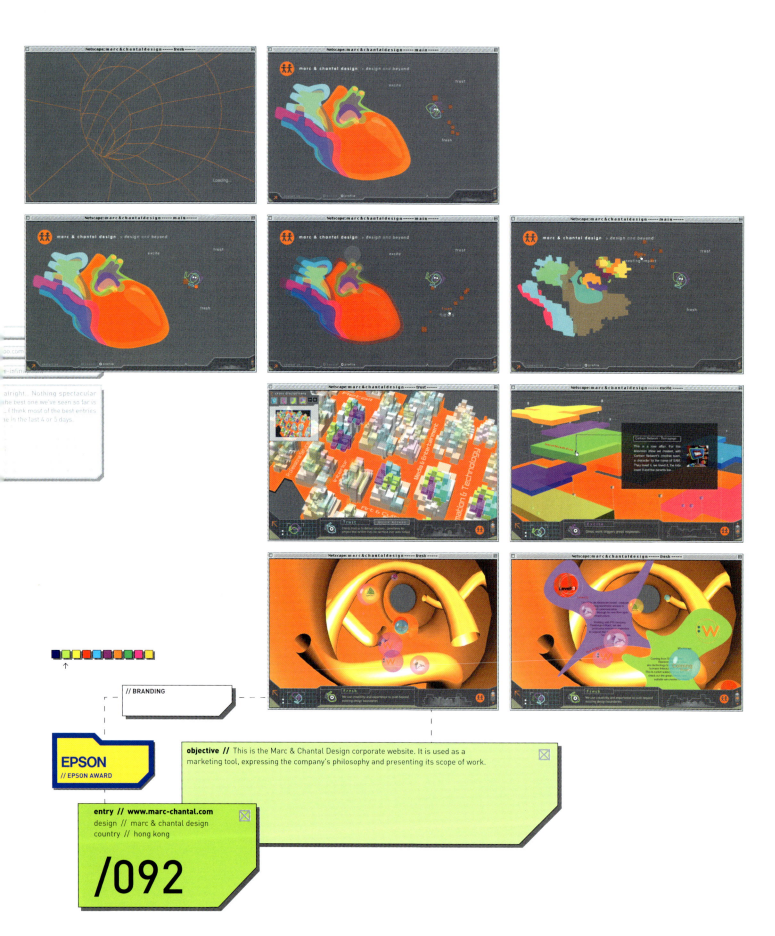

EPSON
// EPSON AWARD

objective // This is the Marc & Chantal Design corporate website. It is used as a marketing tool, expressing the company's philosophy and presenting its scope of work.

entry // www.marc-chantal.com
design // marc & chantal design
country // hong kong

/092

objective // The site was set up at April 1999 as the experiment of the developer. There is no big mission and vision behind this site development, but only the feedback to being drawn by Internet.

entry // www.mars.idv.tw
design // huang mars
country // taiwan

/093

Name: gavinstokes

email: gavinstokes@eircom.net

homepage: http://www.cafe-infinity.com

comment: Nice sites but i think a lot of them have just decided to hell with download times (and im on a ISDN)

WELCOME TO YOWOOYA!®

e@hananet.net

y.dreamwiz.com/tears4me

ching! machanic factory image with
und——um! I've got 21 point at the intro

// HIGHER EDUCATION

objective // It is a Flash site, which is serving as a personal showcase. With the columns, namely "my gallery" which feature the cartoon character created by the site owner and "about me", which provide a detailed profile, visitors could know more about the developer and her works as well.

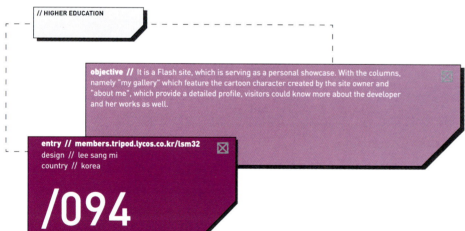

entry // members.tripod.lycos.co.kr/lsm32
design // lee sang mi
country // korea

/094

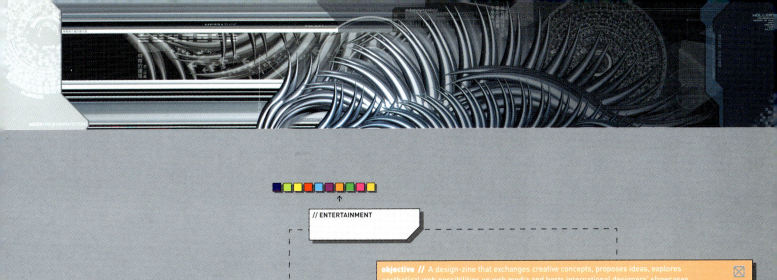

// ENTERTAINMENT

objective // A design-zine that exchanges creative concepts, proposes ideas, explores aesthetical web possibilities on web media and hosts international designers' showcases. It focuses on flash's design and communication capability within the Asian arena with the Western Flash community. I would like this to be the Flash design portal.

entry // www.mezzatype.com
design // patric chua
country // singapore

/095

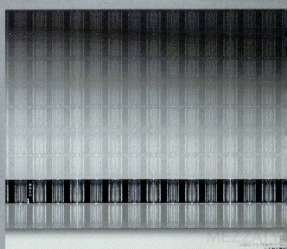

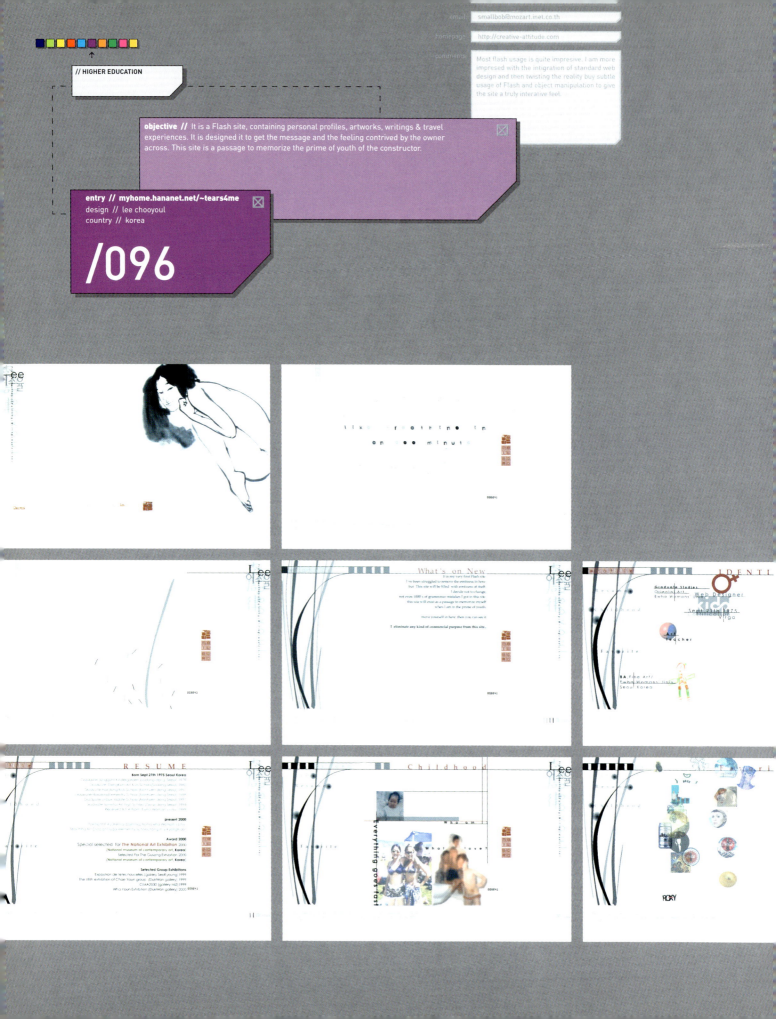

email // smallbob1@mozart.inet.co.th

homepage // http://creative-attitude.com

comments // Most flash usage is quite impresive. I am more impressed with the intigration of standard web design and then twisting the reality buy subtle usage of Flash and object manipulation to give the site a truly interative feel.

objective // It is a Flash site, containing personal profiles, artworks, writings & travel experiences. It is designed it to get the message and the feeling contrived by the owner across. This site is a passage to memorize the prime of youth of the constructor.

entry // myhome.hananet.net/~tears4me
design // lee chooyoul
country // korea

/096

 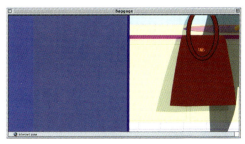 

 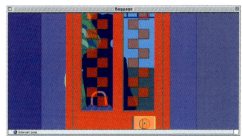 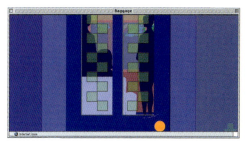

// ENTERTAINMENT

objective // Baggage is a non-linear story about the lives of three women. Lies, guilt, betrayal and grief are examined by looking at the contents of the women's handbags. Contrasting the women's own statements about themselves, overheard through a crack in a door, with the information discernible in the handbags, allows you to discover their real story.

entry // www.neroliwesley.com.au/baggage/
design // neroli wesley (animation and interactive media of rmit university)
country // australia

/097

m	read	question	ask	answer	visit	see	hear	smell	taste	feel	remember
talk	sing	skip	think	ponder	contemplate	lift	drop	grab	throw	catch	t
wnload	search	choose	join	submit	reset	sign up	delay	blush	flourish	smil
connect	stop	start	climb	penetrate	withdraw	lower	yank	crank	wank	tear
lapse	pause	test	bulge	confuse	plot	win	wear	reciprocate	interrupt	st
tap	scatch	pick	step	wash	hug	scrub	make	destroy	create	yell	scream
ommiserate	launch	project	extend	expand	display	return	discard	continue	quit
grovel	kiss	embrace	eat	repel	come	cum	discharge	ejaculate	call	receive
ully	butcher	duplicate	eliminate	circulate	clip	anger	dream	imagine	visualize
eed	bend	cry	weep	shake	rock	roll	vomit	exorcise	press	dump	gulp
eive	consent	decree	lie	intersect	condense	condone	finish	memorize	consider
pull	poke	wave	bow	smoke	repeat	stutter	whisper	hunt	smuggle	liqu
ok	add	subtract	multiply	divide	seperate	divorce	unite	mold	select	sketch
contaminate	clean	decorate	decide	conclude	rap	wrap	get	ram	strangle	put
merize	employ	engage	rent	surprise	hijack	compel	draw	paint	bleed	merge
arrel	argue	shove	promote	fondle	leave	work	pursue	purge	kill	pulsate
ep	mark	lust	nurture	care	incubate	indemnify	hum	hunger	crave	resolve
oscure	obliterate	annihilate	eradicate	erase	remove	rub	stroke	caress	announce
rest	sleep	restart	trim	truncate	conquer	prevail	whip	chill	tie	flirt
at	retire	crash	flop	flip	hit	begrudge	tackle	shoot	arrive	depart	embar
ute	hail	respect	accost	⁙	respond	reply	meditate	entertain	rotate	revolve
andle	grope	fumble	grip	grumble	growl	guess	chew	reap	sow	hang	c
o	assist	reserve	save	earn	exult	own	linger	plant	covet	wish	slouch
nger	plant	covet	wish	slouch	sprawl	prosecute	defend	stagger	enjoy	savor
i	verify	validate	pour	lay	trip	taunt	reap	sow	hang	conceal	show
se	torment	teach	instruct	gossip	use	exploit	upset	aim	uproot	help	ass
steal	free	feed	confess	tickle	fart	handle	grope	fumble	grip	grumble	s
salute	hail	accost	greet	respond	reply	meditate	entertain	rotate	revolve	deli
bark	embellish	eject	elect	offer	give	stroke	caress	announce	cough	testify
revive	faint	retain	replace	illustrate	renew	pay	rest	sleep	restart	resolve
scure	obliterate	annihilate	find	eradicate	erase	remove	rub	pursue	purge	ki
drift	float	roam	record	measure	maximize	minimize	match	watch	keep	ma
pass	tame	pet	quench	quell	restrain	extinguish	suppress	write	gag	belie
ibit	boast	fascinate	mesmerize	employ	engage	rent	surprise	hijack	compel
econtaminate	clean	decorate	decide	conclude	rap	wrap	get	ram	strangle	pu
ultiply	divide	seperate	divorce	unite	surmise	obfuscate	obey	contort	oblige
ect	behave	choke	burp	rectify	sweat	pluck	force	jam	cram	carry	drool
cupy	study	view	perceive	consent	decree	lie	intersect	condescend	transfer
eed	bend	cry	weep	shake	rock	roll	vomit	exorcise	press	dump	gulp
magine	visualize	enlighten	inspire	illuminate	demonstrate	strip	bully	butcher	di
crawl	beg	grovel	kiss	embrace	eat	repel	come	cum	discharge	ejacula
tend	expand	display	return	abide	endure	laugh	jettison	harmonize	query	u
n	hug	scrub	make	destroy	create	yell	scream	buy	connect	sell	order
ose	pause	test	bulge	confuse	plot	act	envy	perform	realize	satisfy	sett
rip	leap	swim	pounce	cut	copy	throw	catch	lose	talk	turn	raise

ist | analyze | forget | synthesize | drink | suck | push | waste | recharge | emulate | und

raise | hold | release | switch | pontificate | ramble | scrutinize | breathe | live | die | dis

mirk | reduce | serve | act | envy | perform | realize | satisfy | settle | neglect | violate

leap | swim | dive | pounce | cut | copy | paste | clear | drive | shit | speak | fly

yawn | corrupt | suspend | abide | endure | laugh | jettison | harmonize | query | understan

uy | sell | order | hide | seek | reveal | play | sink | do | mix | fuck | drag | crawl

art | accomodate | agree | accomplish | commit | enlighten | inspire | illuminate | demonstrate

stretch | screw | fill | twirl | spin | shout | simulate | scrape | ache | yearn | want

escend | transfer | bounce | dismiss | expel | evict | boycott | terminate | occupy | study

llow | sweat | pluck | force | jam | cram | carry | drool | swat | slap | smack | break

serve | preserve | protect | surmise | obfuscate | obey | contort | oblige | condemn | abando

hustle | support | affect | behave | choke | burp | rectify | fix | judge | die | declare

udge | neutralize | hump | nod | notify | itch | thirst | hop | squeeze | inhibit | boast

bdue | succumb | tame | pet | quench | quell | restrain | extinguish | suppress | write | ga

lend | suffer | have | drift | float | roam | record | measure | maximize | minimize | match

throb | shrink | grow | program | type | edit | correct | reproduce | pelt | rush | pa

or | inquire | pray | punish | participate | interact | retain | replace | illustrate | disconnect

gh | testify | publish | cuddle | moan | groan | pant | become | change | flatter | conform

crush | resurrect | revive | faint | burn | triumph | restore | diminish | comfort | tolerate

mbellish | eject | elect | offer | give | take | borrow | steal | free | feed | confess | tick

liberate | reflect | tease | torment | teach | instruct | gossip | use | exploit | upset | aim

show | harass | harm | hate | despise | love | adore | worship | cherish | treasure | s

wl | prosecute | defend | stagger | enjoy | savor | impose | liberate | let | approve | allow

pose | liberate | let | approve | allow | load | build | verify | validate | pour | lay | tri

harm | hate | despise | love | adore | worship | cherish | treasure | slip | fall | take

reserve | save | earn | exult | own | burn | triumph | restore | diminish | comfort | tolera

guess | chew | retire | crash | flop | flip | hit | begrudge | tackle | shoot | arrive

reflect | trim | truncate | conquer | prevail | whip | chill | tie | flirt | wink | crush

lish | cuddle | moan | groan | pant | become | change | flatter | conform | resist | beat

ct | honor | inquire | pray | punish | participate | interact | bleed | merge | blend | suffer

ulsate | bloom | throb | shrink | grow | program | type | edit | correct | reproduce | pelt

lust | nurture | care | incubate | indemnify | hum | hunger | crave | itch | thirst | hop

quarrel | argue | shove | promote | fondle | leave | work | fix | judge | die | declare

paint | mold | select | sketch | smudge | neutralize | hump | nod | notify | cook | add

bdue | succumb | smoke | repeat | stutter | whisper | hunt | smuggle | liquefy | hustle

un | abandon | trap | condense | condone | finish | memorize | consider | conserve | preserv

wat | slap | smack | break | thrust | pull | poke | wave | bow | ache | yearn | want

dismiss | expel | evict | boycott | terminate | duplicate | eliminate | circulate | clip | ang

llow | stretch | screw | fill | twirl | spin | shout | simulate | scrape | sink | do | mix

continue | quit | restart | accomodate | agree | accomplish | commit | commiserate | launch

all | receive | kick | paste | clear | drive | shit | speak | fly | blink | tap | scatch | p

nd | attend | win | wear | reciprocate | interrupt | stain | yawn | corrupt | suspend | cance

seek | reveal | play | stop | start | climb | penetrate | withdraw | lower | yank | cran

eglect | violate | delay | blush | flourish | smile | smirk | reduce | serve | go | download

release | switch | pontificate | ramble | scrutinize | breathe | live | die | move | design

objective // It's an entertainment website. So I wanted to create something spectacular for the design. I wanted to merge scripting with design to create something awesome, to create something that would entertain.

entry // www.netshelter.net
design // mchael worobec
country // australia

/100

Name: Sonny

email: sunny@dangero

link 1: http://drpag.virt

comments: Kewl macromed.rwebdesign site, but where are all the entries?

Have i missed anything? Only one entry from amoeba?

anways, page is not quite impressive.

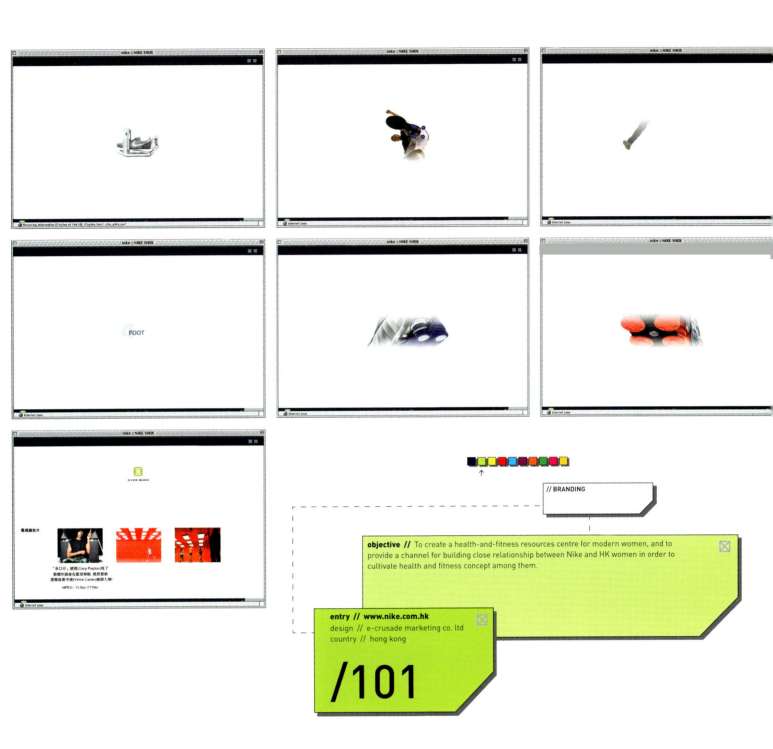

// BRANDING

objective // To create a health-and-fitness resources centre for modern women, and to provide a channel for building close relationship between Nike and HK women in order to cultivate health and fitness concept among them.

entry // www.nike.com.hk
design // e-crusade marketing co. ltd
country // hong kong

/101

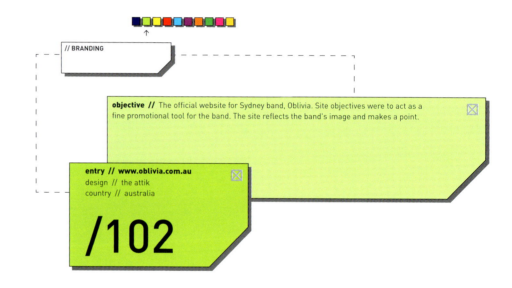

// BRANDING

objective // The official website for Sydney band, Oblivia. Site objectives were to act as a fine promotional tool for the band. The site reflects the band's image and makes a point.

entry // www.oblivia.com.au
design // the attik
country // australia

/102

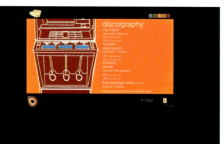

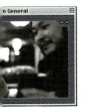

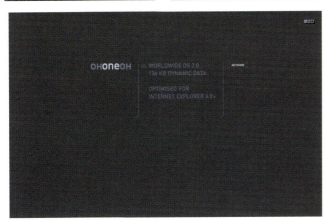

objective // OH | ONE | OH is a collective of passionate problem-solvers based in Beijing, China. The site is designed to reflect an "Operative System". Since some of us have Scandinavian roots, we opt for solutions that are functional and minimalist. The site is targeted at existing and possible clients. So it is key that our identity and presence on the web is direct, informative and to the point. ☒

entry // www.ohoneoh.com ☒
design // oh | one | oh
country // china

/103

// BRANDING

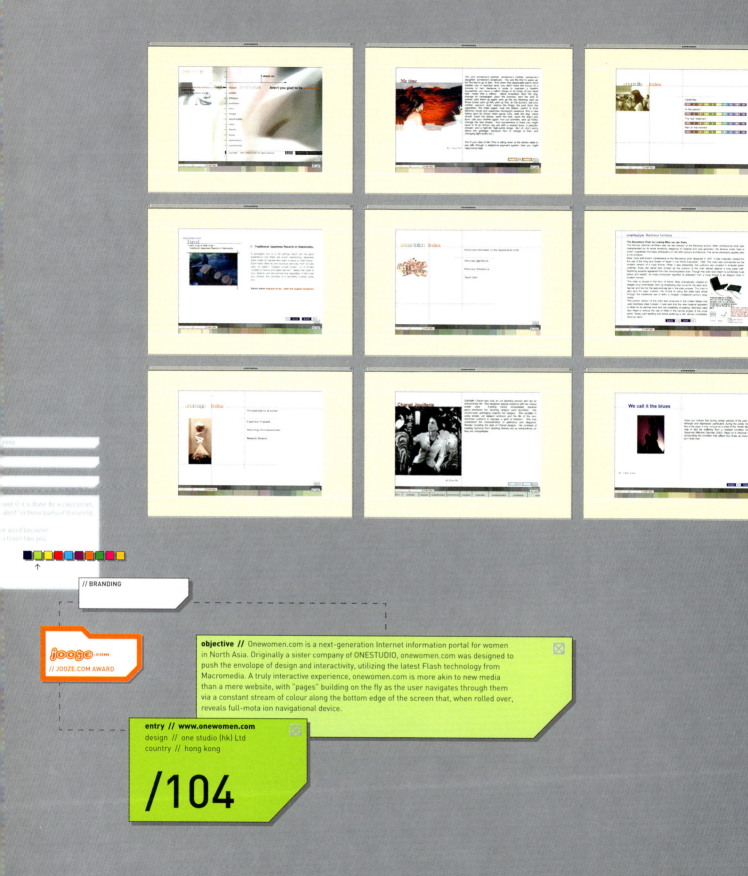

// BRANDING

objective // Onewomen.com is a next-generation Internet information portal for women in North Asia. Originally a sister company of ONESTUDIO, onewomen.com was designed to push the envolope of design and interactivity, utilizing the latest Flash technology from Macromedia. A truly interactive experience, onewomen.com is more akin to new media than a mere website, with "pages" building on the fly as the user navigates through them via a constant stream of colour along the bottom edge of the screen that, when rolled over, reveals full-mota ion navigational device.

entry // www.onewomen.com
design // one studio (hk) Ltd
country // hong kong

/104

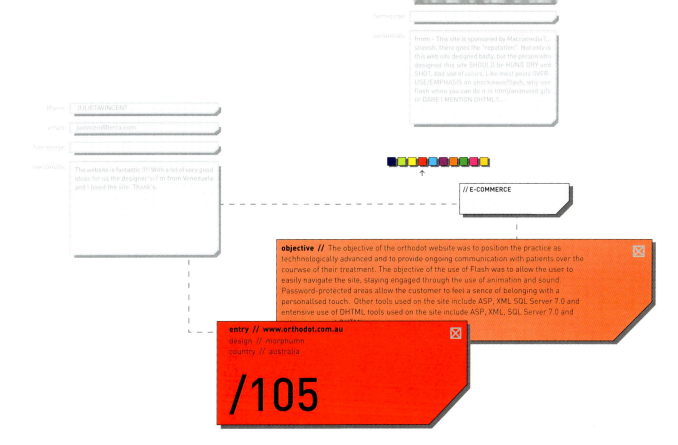

// E-COMMERCE

objective // The objective of the orthodot website was to position the practice as
techhnologically advanced and to provide ongoing communication with patients over the
courwse of their treatment. The objective of the use of Flash was to allow the user to
easily navigate the site, staying engaged through the use of animation and sound.
Password-protected areas allow the customer to feel a sence of belonging with a
personallsed touch. Other tools used on the site include ASP, XML SQL Server 7.0 and
entensive use of DHTML tools used on the site include ASP, XML, SQL Server 7.0 and

entry // www.orthodot.com.au
design // morphumn
country // australia

/105

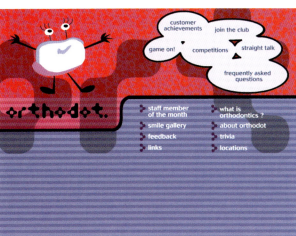

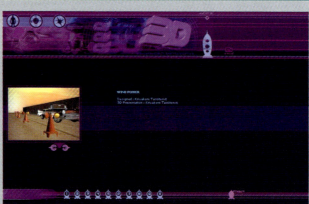

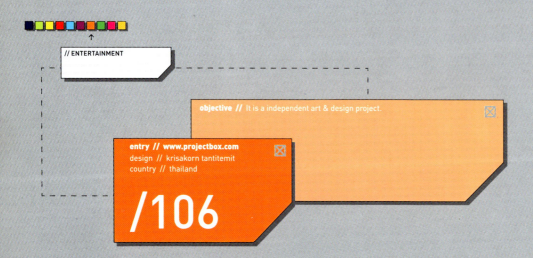

// ENTERTAINMENT

objective // It is a independent art & design project.

entry // www.projectbox.com
design // krisakorn tantitemit
country // thailand

/106

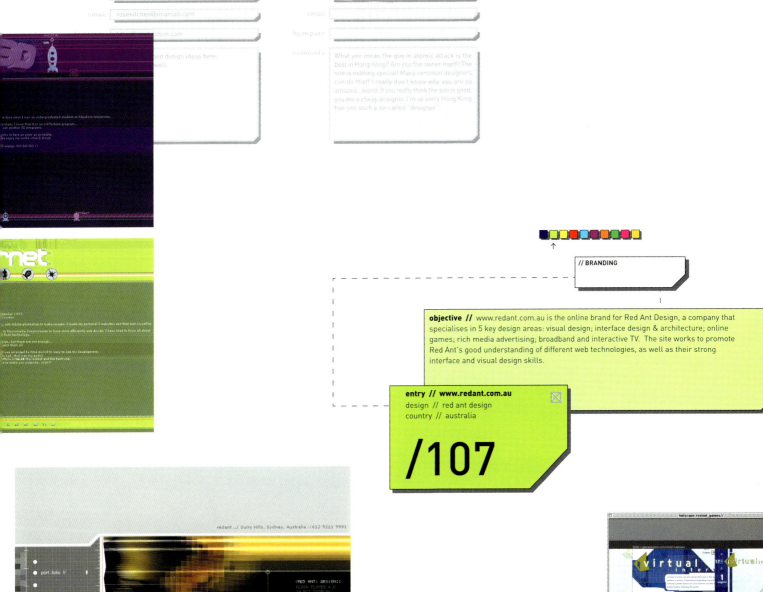

// BRANDING

objective // www.redant.com.au is the online brand for Red Ant Design, a company that specialises in 5 key design areas: visual design; interface design & architecture; online games; rich media advertising; broadband and interactive TV. The site works to promote Red Ant's good understanding of different web technologies, as well as their strong interface and visual design skills.

entry // www.redant.com.au
design // red ant design
country // australia

/107

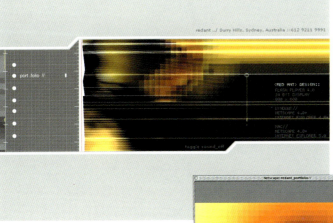

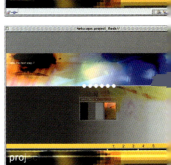

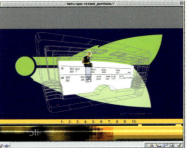

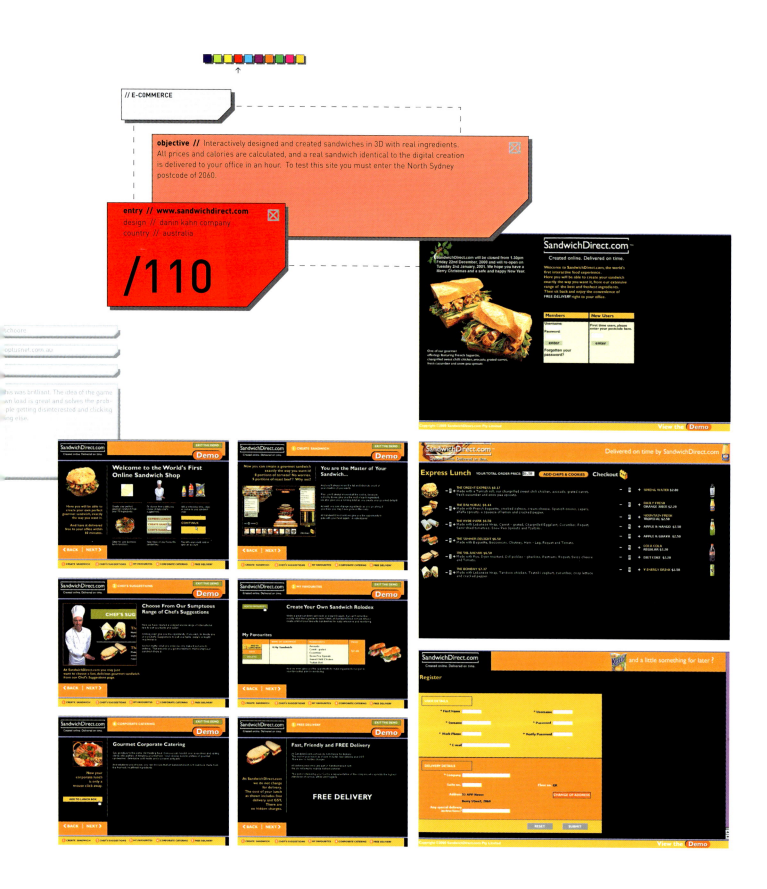

// E-COMMERCE

objective // Interactively designed and created sandwiches in 3D with real ingredients. All prices and calories are calculated, and a real sandwich identical to the digital creation is delivered to your office in an hour. To test this site you must enter the North Sydney postcode of 2060.

entry // www.sandwichdirect.com
design // danin kahn company
country // australia

/110

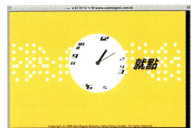

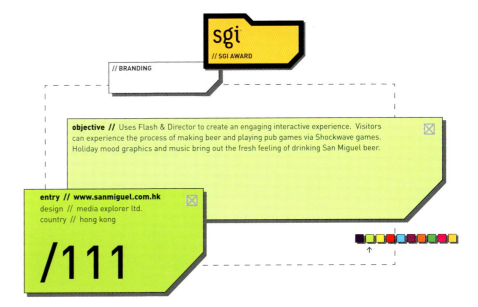

sgi

// SGI AWARD

// BRANDING

objective // Uses Flash & Director to create an engaging interactive experience. Visitors can experience the process of making beer and playing pub games via Shockwave games. Holiday mood graphics and music bring out the fresh feeling of drinking San Miguel beer.

entry // www.sanmiguel.com.hk
design // media explorer ltd.
country // hong kong

/111

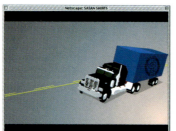

// E-COMMERCE

objective // Satan Shirts is an e-commerce site built around a fictional character called the Big Devil. The site currently offers merchandise for sale from Auckland alternative radio station 95bFM. In the future, users will be able to submit their own designs to the site for consideration, and other lines of merchandise will also be offered.

entry // www.satanshirts.com
design // webmedia
country // new zealand

/112

objective // For 50 years Harry Seidler has played a vital role in international architecture. His work is widely recognised as an original and intensely creative contribution to the architecture of the second half of the 20th Century. This website is targeted at potential clients, as well as acting as an online resource for architectural academics/historians and students of Modernism.

// E-BUSINESS

entry // www.seidler.net.au
design // gary venter
country // australia

/113

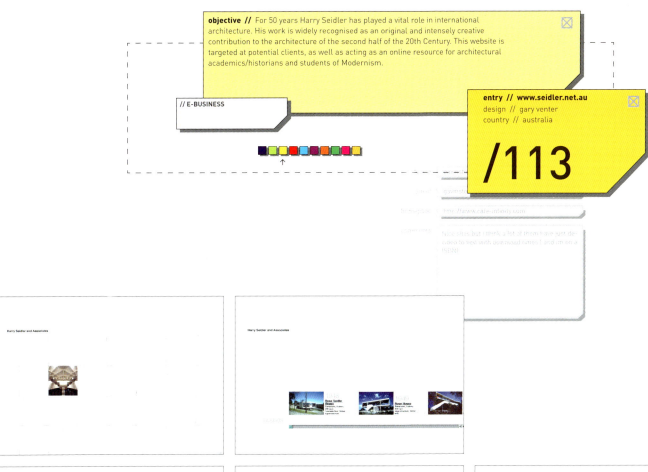

// HIGHER EDUCATION

objective // seoleuan.com designed and created for more interactive communication between creator & users on the Internet.

entry // www.seoleuna.com
design // eun-a seol
country // korea

/114

[G-L-a-n-c-e]

everything is a play

OUT PLAN LONGIN

>unlimited

Enjoy Yourself with seoleuna.Com

www seoleuna com

It has only just started to meet You and I.

// BRANDING

objective // CNET Singapore (singapore.cnet.com) is Singapore's source for technology and computers, providing international content from CNET to complement and complete the unparalleled breadth of our local coverage. CNET Singapore is the definitive Internet content site on technology news and information, linking buyers and sellers online. CNET Singapore sends over 310,000 newsletters monthly to its subscribers and registers over 150,000 unique monthly visitors at the site.

entry // www.singapore.cnet.com
design // asiacontent.com media pte ltd
country // singapore

/115

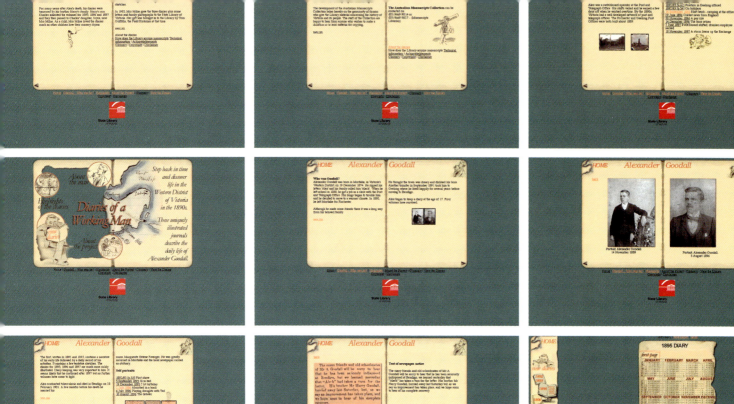

// GOVERNMENT

objective // This website explains the significance of the diaries and places them in the context of the history of the Geelong area. The objectives of the site are: To provide ready access to unique and fragile manuscripts. To make regional material (in this case Geelong) available locally via the web. To publish an interesting online exhibition based on a significant heritage item.

entry // www.slv.vic.gov.au/slv/exhibitions/diaries/
design // state library of victoria
country // australia

/116

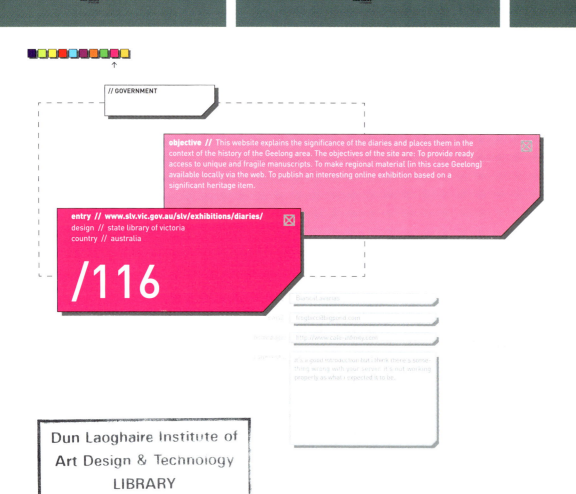

skip intro

// CORPORATE TRAINING

objective // The Sydney Opera House Kids site is essentially an educational site for children. Games revolved around information about the Opera House are designed to evoke children is interest in visiting again. It is also development on the characters from the Kids Events Shows, that run during the course of the Sydney Opera House's 'Kids' theatrical season. You will need to use the password; "Spike" in the "Secret Kids Stuff" section.

entry // www.soh.nsw.gov.au/files/calendar/kids/kids.html
design // fizzy cactus
country // australia

/117

THE RESISTANCE OF MINORITY

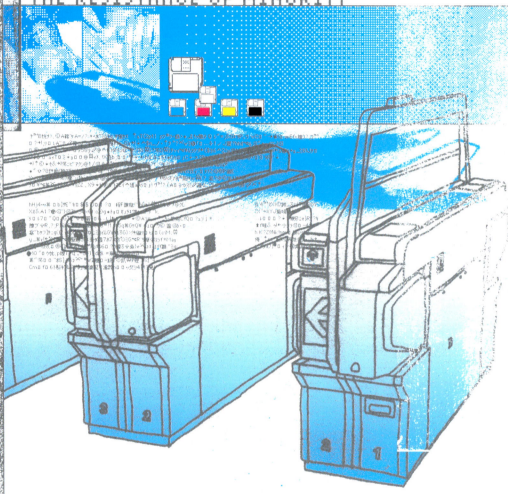

objective // spike.com is a website about music, video, radio and and TV. in the site, visitors can enjoy the games and give vs their feedback.

entry // www.spike.com
design // spike cyberworks
country // australia

/120

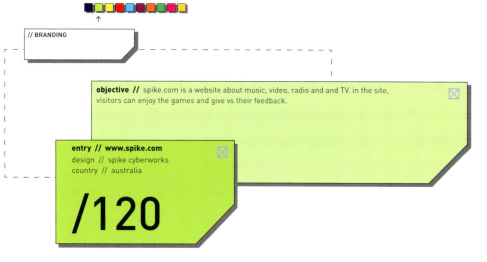

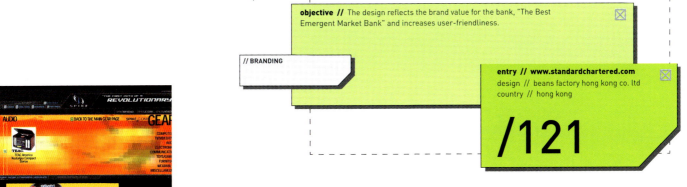

objective // The design reflects the brand value for the bank, "The Best Emergent Market Bank" and increases user-friendliness.

// BRANDING

entry // www.standardchartered.com
design // beans factory hong kong co. ltd
country // hong kong

/121

skip intro

skip intro
skip intro

// E-COMMERCE

objective // Spongestore is an international online boutique offering a unique and directional range of products and services. Its aim is to become the pre-eminent destination in this field. The unique range of products cannot be found at a single retail or e-tail location anywhere around the world.

entry // www.spongestore.com
design // citrus internet
country // australia

/122

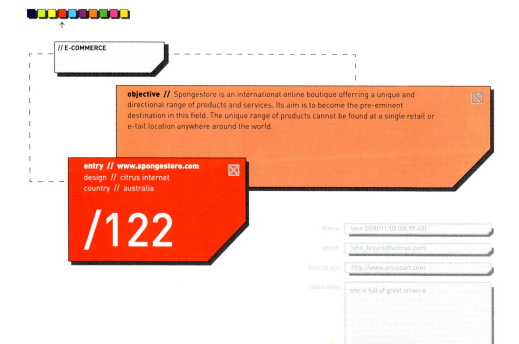

objective // Presents streaming services and builds up streamingasia limited image.

// e-BUSINESS

entry // www.streamingasia.com
design // logicspace limited
country // hong kong

/123

objective // The Subaru Australia features extensive personalisation and self-service. The objective were to further build and extend the brand on-line by communicating key brand benefits that could be represented effectively in other mediums.

entry // www.subaru.com.au
design // leo burnett
country // australia

/124

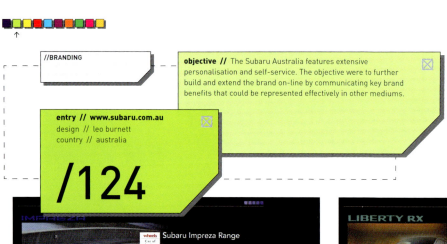

objective // TAB is New Zealand's largest online gaming organization. The site features the Real Audio feed from Trackside, which supplies live commentary via the site on New Zealand races, along with a broadcasting schedule for the current day is racing. And then there is the online betting facility. The back-end betting engine supplied by Australian firm eBet allows users to set up a gaming account, place bets and track results.

entry // www.tab.co.nz
design // zivo new zealand limited
country // new zealand

// E-BUSINESS

/125

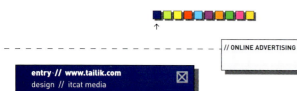

// ONLINE ADVERTISING

entry·// www.tailik.com
design // itcat media
country // hong kong

/126

objective // Entertainment Portal hosted by the hottest comedy movie director in Hong Kong, Mr Lee Lik Chee. Extensive use of grahics and animation uses over 2000 pages of information. Makes it stand apart from other portal site.

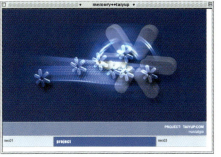

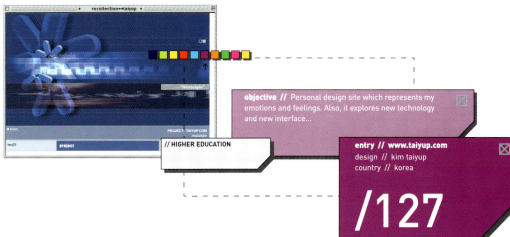

objective // Personal design site which represents my emotions and feelings. Also, it explores new technology and new interface...

// HIGHER EDUCATION

entry // www.taiyup.com
design // kim taiyup
country // korea

/127

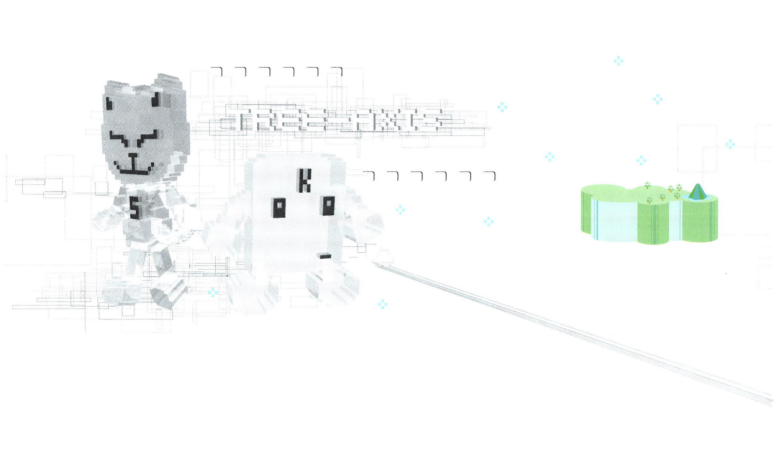

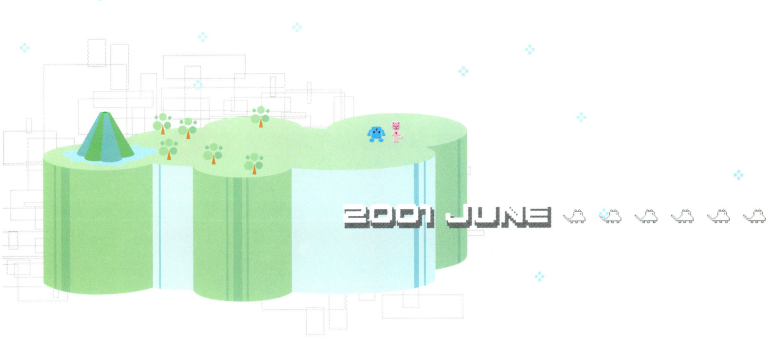

2001 JUNE

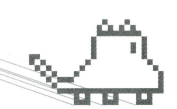

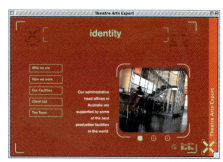

objective // Theatre Arts Export produces staging & live events across Australia and Asia. Nectarine chose Flash to create an online experience that would reflect the presence and quality of Theatre Arts Export. The site utilizes a powerful database, driven internally from Flash, to generate menus and display projects.

// E-BUSINESS

entry // www.theatrearts-export.com
design // nectarine
country // australia

/130

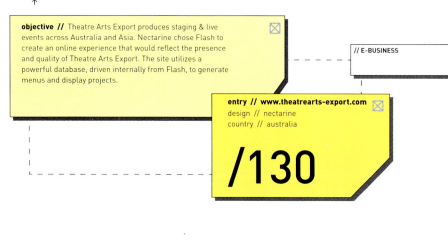

objective // toyota.com enables its visitors to know more about Toyota, both the company and also its car, through various columns, namely "inside Toyota", "Motorsports", "Toyactive" and "used vehicle search".

entry // www.toyota.com.au
design // spike cyberworks
country // australia

/131

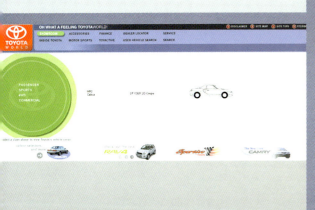

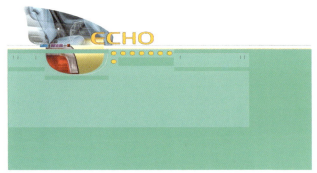

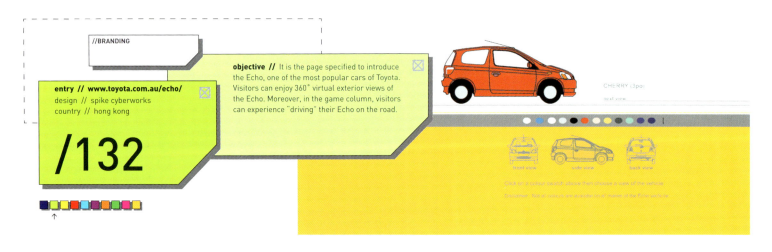

//BRANDING

entry // www.toyota.com.au/echo/
design // spike cyberworks
country // hong kong

/132

objective // It is the page specified to introduce the Echo, one of the most popular cars of Toyota. Visitors can enjoy 360° virtual exterior views of the Echo. Moreover, in the game column, visitors can experience "driving" their Echo on the road.

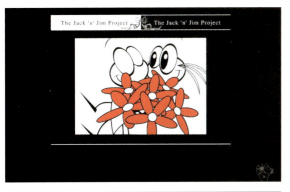

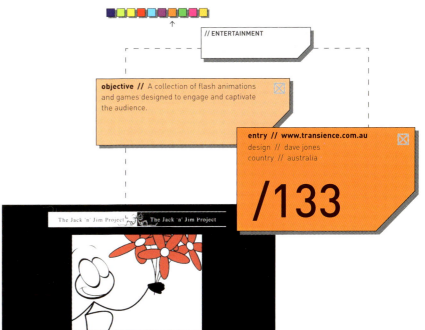

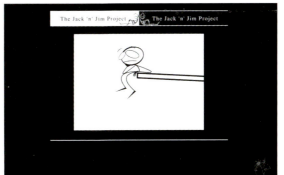

objective // Online portfolio for Urban Buffalo Provides our
current and potential clients with a view of our work, clients,
capabilities and methodology. The site demonstrates our
online capabilities.

// BRANDING

entry // www.urban-buffalo.com
design // urban buffalo creative
country // australia

/134

objective // This site was designed to promote the Australian launch of the new Motorola V2288 mobile phone. The main objective was to showcase the features of the phone, and create an excitment about the product in the eyes of the target audience (15-25 year olds).

// ONLINE ADVERTISING

entry // www.v2288.com.au
design // reactive media
country // australia

/135

Name: huiyonuglee 2000/09/29 (23:40:12)
email: purina_man@yahoo.co.kr
homepage: http://odora.hihome.com
comments: i.. korean highschool student. my dream is webdesigner. this site concept is freedom.

Name: juju 2000/09/29 (06:03:45)
email:
homepage:
comments: great design very *!! (wallpaper.co.uk
nice clean work none of this animatio
mations sake.
Only thing is scroll bars are very
iritating... I can understand if you are
designing for abstract space ie

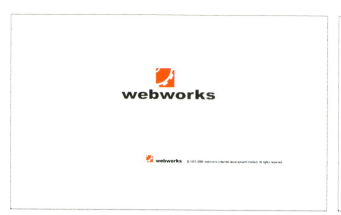

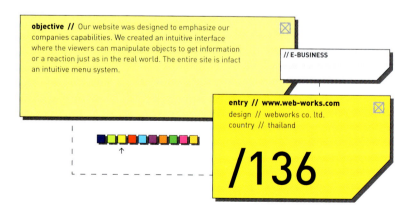
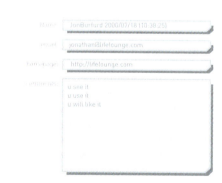

objective // Our website was designed to emphasize our companies capabilities. We created an intuitive interface where the viewers can manipulate objects to get information or a reaction just as in the real world. The entire site is infact an intuitive menu system.

// E-BUSINESS

entry // www.web-works.com
design // webworks co. ltd.
country // thailand

/136

homepage: http://www.suture.net

comments: nice site

webworks

browsing
an employee
a client

click the visitors book for access

webworks © 1997-2000 webworks internet development limited. All rights reserved.

interview our clients to gather
mation from them regarding their aims
objectives.

sk them to fill in one of our
stionnaires which help us to focus the
ct around the main requirements of
business.

webworks © 1997-2000 webworks internet development limited. All rights reserved.

// ONLINE ADVERTISING

objective // Affice.com's online advertising & design site.
Webbee World introduces various designs about Webbee of
Affice.com to the world. Through this site, the world can see
the LastOne's Design capacity, and many users are able to
learn about Macromedia Flash in Korea.

entry // www.webbee.co.kr
design // lastone inc.
country // korea

/137

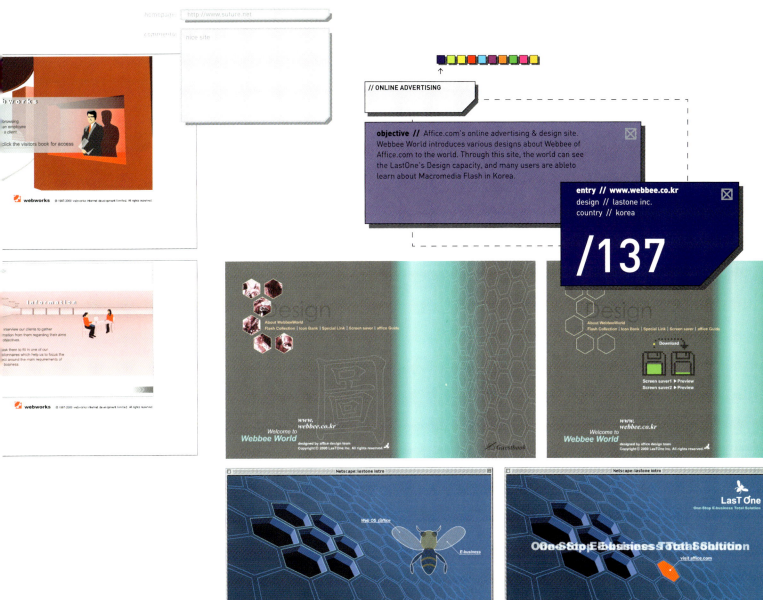

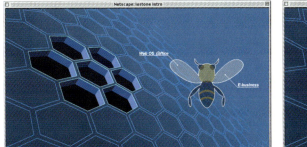

Name: digerati 2000/07/14 (11:03:50)

email: digerati@hotmail.com

homepage: http://www.ericsson.com.hk

comments: When web met phone can be so cool. When content met technology can be that beautiful.

a chock full of

00 pictures and
, college life,
ican.

objective // Taking the role of the Coca-Cola polar bear, to accumulate as much refreshing Coca-Cola as possible. A Flash movie shows the bear jumping onto an ice floe as he heads from Alaska to Singapore. An route, he goes fishing with his magnet lure to grasp cans, bottles and six-packs. Each has a separate value and the more he reels in and put in your trusty Coca-Cola cooler, the more points you get. There are numerous enemies in the deep who will break his line so they can keep the Coke for themselves. As time passes, the ice floe moves on the warmer waters of Hawaii and eventually Singapore. If the bear makes it to Singapore, he is able to deliver his bounty to his thirsty family in the tropical island.

entry // xm-folio.com/coca-cola/
ice_fishing_splash.shtml
design // ccg.xm pte ltd
country // singapore

/138

// ENTERTAINMENT

The website is fantastic !!!! With a lot of very good ideas for us the designer's. I'm from Venezuela and I loved the site. Thank's. • cokebuddy website is the best Australian macromedia website. Thanx Macromedia for making the cokebuddy the best looking site on the web. • I think its an attractive clean & impressive corporate site. • yep, it's true that it's a nice website.

Name: OndreaBarbe 2000/09/10 (11:01:59)

email: info@ondreabarbe.com

homepage: http://www.ondreabarbe.com

comments: I would like to submit my site for consideration. Thank you

The Coca-Cola Polar Bar

The Coca-Cola Polar Bar
game over

Play again   Quit

objective // All the characters in Coca-Cola web-based Polar Bar Game are lovable polar bears in various stages of winter dress. The user plays the bartender who waits for customers to wander into his establishment. As each customer sits down, they are served a tall glass of Coca-Cola. It is the bartender's task to use his tap to keep each glass from being emptied. As time goes by, more and more patrons enter and the bartender must keep on his toes to make sure no one is neglected. Once three glasses are empty, the game ends.

// ENTERTAINMENT

entry // m-folio.com/coca-cola/
polar_bar_splash.shtml
design // ccg.xm pte ltd
country // singapore

/139

objective // The site aims at giving its audience something fun, but also something that is useful. Desktop post, something new but growing in popularity seemed an ideal platform for creating branding for Coke. Users simply downloaded an executable file and installed to enjoy the application, which has a range of useful features.

Name : zero 2000/06

email : one_below_

homepage : http://www.t

comments : i really enjoy the graphics

entry // xm-folio.com/coca-cola/
posties_splash.shtml
design // ccg.xm pte ltd
country // singapore

/140

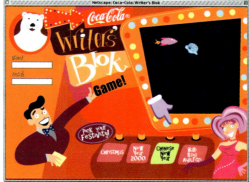

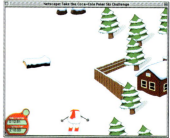

URL	DESIGN	COUNTRY
203.62.157.251	Massive Interactive Pty. Ltd.	Australia
www.3drums.com	3 Drums Limited	Hong Kong
www.52mm.com	52mm/Product52	U.S.A.
www.555.com	555 Design Fabrication Management Inc.	U.S.A.
www.amphibianarc.com	Robyn Sambo	U.S.A.
www.bausch.com.tw/event1/index.htm	Ogilvy Interactive	Taiwan
www.cocopops.com.au	Leo Burnett	Australia
www.ddbi.com.hk/macromedia/CompaqCarRacing/content.html	Tribal DDB Hong Hong	Hong Hong
www.ddbi.com.hk/macromedia/Epson/content.html	Tribal DDB Hong Kong	Hong Kong
www.ddbi.com.hk/macromedia/SCMPBanner/stock/index.html	Tribal DDB Hong Kong	Hong Kong
www.digitallime.com	Digital Lime Pty. Ltd.	Australia
www.digitforce.com	Digitforce Interactive Design Studio	Hong Kong
www.duskvalley.com/vis-dom	Dusk Valley Technologies	India
www.edenstudio.com/kgt/	Eden Studio	Taiwan
www.edenstudio.com/portfolio/HKTgrab/grab.htm	Eden Studio	Taiwan
www.eglue.com.au	Elcom Technology Pty. Ltd.	Australia
ericsson.ht.net.tw	Ogilvy Interactive	Taiwan
ericsson.ht.net.tw/R320	Ogilvy Interactive	Taiwan
www.europe.com.hk	1stop-toys.com	Hong Kong
eventplay.acergame.com.tw/motorola/index.html	Acer Internet Services Inc.	Taiwan
www.eye4u.com	Kunal Kuthiala	India
www.gecapital.com.hk	Modem Media (HK) Limited	Hong Kong
www.globalplus.co.nz	ZIVO New Zealand Limited	New Zealand
www.goo.idv.tw	Ken Cheng	Taiwan
www.healthnwealthnow.com	Mike Hoste	Australia
www.hkacnt.com	Forecast Media	Hong Kong
www.icommercialnet.com	I-CommercialNet Limited	Hong Kong
www.i-dore.com	i-dore Co. Ltd.	Hong Kong
www.intrasync.com	IntraSync (Private) Limited	Pakistan
www.jamesbond.com/intro_flash.html	Edmund B Flading IV	U.S.A.
members.nbci.com/hwangstudio/loopmaster	Lok Kerk Hwang	Singapore
www.mymbassy.com	Leo Burnett	Australia
mypage.channeli.net/sunny	Design Mind	Korea
playzone.acergame.com.tw/event/weblympics/	Acer Internet Services Inc.	Taiwan
www.reinhardtdesign.net	reinhardtdesign.net	germany
www.renu.com.tw	Ogilvy Interactive	Taiwan
www.spin.com.au	Spin New Media	Australia
www.sunday.com/sunday/Portal?xml=cupid/home	Modem Media (HK) Limited	Hong Kong
www.tailik.com/	ITCAT Media	Hong Kong
www.toyota.com.au	Spike CyberWorks	Australia
www.twice2.ch	Johann Terrettaz	Switzerland
www.v2288.com.au	Reactive Media	Australia

// online advertising

URL	DESIGN	COUNTRY
www.vw.com.mx	Gedas North America	Mexico
www.webbee.co.kr	LasTOne Inc.	Korea
xm-folio.com/coca-cola/posties_splash.shtml	CCG.XM Pte Ltd	Singapore
xm-folio.com/compaq/armada100s/index.html	CCG.XM Pte Ltd	Singapore
xm-folio.com/compaq/deskprosb/index.html	CCG.XM Pte Ltd	Singapore
xm-folio.com/compaq/screensaver/download.html	CCG.XM Pte Ltd	Singapore

// branding

URL	DESIGN	COUNTRY
www.4everything.co.kr	Kim Won Hee	Korea
www.95bfm.com	WebMedia	New Zealand
www.acmedia.net	Acmedia (S) Pte Ltd	Singapore
www.aidio.com	Aidio Multimedia Assassins	U.S.A.
www.amoeba.com.sg	Amoeba Media	Singapore
www.avlight.com	爱浪國際	China
www.bausch.com.tw	Ogilvy Interactive	Taiwan
www.baycrest.com.hk	Pacificlink iMedia Ltd	Hong Kong
www.bee-net.com	BEENET	Hong Kong
www.belcher.com.hk/	Stephen Lo	Hong Kong
www.billabong.com	WEB Twentyone.Com	Australia
www.billabong.nestle.com.au	Massive Interactive Pty Ltd	Australia
www.bmw.co.uk/z8	AKQA New Media	U.K.
www.bullhound.com	Elcom Technology Pty Ltd	Australia
www.carltoncold.com.au	Spin New Media	Australia
www.centralhk.com	One Studio (HK) Ltd	Hong Kong
www.channelv.com.au/games/pizzahaven/pizzahaven_game.html	Massive Interactive Pty Ltd	Australia
www.charliebrownonline.com	Spin New Media	Australia
www.choiceworkshop.com	Benny Wang	China
www.clubhotel.com	The Web Connection	Hong Kong
www.colonydesign.com	Colony Design	U.S.A.
www.colour18.com	Media Explorer Ltd.	Hong Kong
www.crankmedia.com.au	Crank Media	Australia
www.db-db.com	Francis Lam	Hong Kong
www.ddbi.com.hk/macromedia/jf/content.htm	Tribal DDB Hong Kong	Hong Kong
www.ddbi.com.hk/macromedia/sony/content.htm	Tribal DDB Hong Kong	Hong Kong
www.ddbi.com.hk/macromedia/vlinkglobal/content.htm	Tribal DDB Hong Kong	Hong Kong
www.ddbi.com.hk/macromedia/VWsite/content.html	Tribal DDB Hong Kong	Hong Kong
www.delapse.com	Delapse Broadcast Design and Animation	South Africa
www.digitalink.com.au	Ray Langmaid	Australia
www.dilbies.com	Schizophrenic Pty Ltd	Australia
www.dreamart.com	Kim Ji Young	Korea
www.e-axis.com	E-axis.com Inc.	Canada

URL	DESIGN	COUNTRY
www.edgematrix.com/creative	EdgeMatrix Pte. Ltd.	Singapore
www.edlinkol.com	Edlink Online Limited	Hong Kong
www.educate.com	Gr8	U.S.A.
elta.com.tw	愛爾達科技股份有限公司	Taiwan
www.eureka-digital.com/hnshk/index.asp	Eureka Digital Ltd.	Hong Kong
www.exportgold.com	Shift	New Zealand
www.eyescream.com.au	Eye Scream Graphic Design	Australia
www.fareast.com.sg	Ken Chan	Singapore
www.fareastone.com.tw	Ogilvy Interactive	Taiwan
www.festivalwalk.com.hk	Modem Media (HK) Limited	Hong Kong
www.fingers10.com	Fingers 10 Ltd.	Hong Kong
www.fog.co.kr	Kim Yeon Jung	Korea
www.fonet.co.kr	Park Eun Young	Korea
www.forecastmedia.com	Forecast Media	Hong Kong
www.formul8.com	Formlu8 Media Pte. Ltd.	Singapore
www.fujitsu-pc-asia.com	Latitude Web Pte. Ltd.	Singapore
funland.extra.com.hk	Media Explorer Ltd.	Hong Kong
www.gaygiano.com	Edlink Online Limited	Hong Kong
www.geocities.com/WWWhat_8/anita/index.html	Anita Wong Wai Ying	Hong Kong
www.glassonion.com.au	Danin Kahn	Australia
www.gmd.com.au	Sausage Ltd.	Australia
www.gogo.com	WebMedia	New Zealand
www.goughscat.co.nz	Turing Solutions (Ltd.)	New Zealand
www.halfkilo.com	Halfkilo (HK) Limited	Hong Kong
www.handphoneas.co.kr	Park Ok Hee	Korea
www.hgc.com.hk	Blue Puk Yuk Chun	Hong Kong
www.hungerfordhill.com.au	Spike CyberWorks	Australia
www.ids.com.hk	IDS Co. Ltd.	Hong Kong
www.imagefactory-group.com	形像工場傳播設計	China
www.islandeast.com.hk	Modem Media (HK) Limited	Hong Kong
www.ilcatmedia.com	ILCAT Media	Hong Kong
www.ithk.com	Fingers 10 Ltd.	Hong Kong
www.itom.com.cn/yili	內蒙古利賣業	China
www.itprocreation.com	ITpro Cre@tion	Hong Kong
www.iworkshop.com.cn	Workshop China	China
www.izzue.com	izzue.com (Hong Kong) Limited	Hong Kong
www.jacobscreek.com.au	Groundhog Software	Australia
www.jessica-intl.com	Media Explorer Ltd.	Hong Kong
www.kinetic.com.sg	Kinetic Interactive Pte. Ltd.	Singapore
www.koreav.net	Lee Sang Mi	Korea
www.koreea.com	Lee Hyang Joo	Korea
www.koreea.net	Lee Kyung Won	Korea

// branding

URL	DESIGN	COUNTRY
www.landroverworld.com	AKQA New Media	U.K.
www.lindemans.com.au	Spike CyberWorks	Australia
www.lmgold.com	陳郁	China
www.marc-chantal.com	Marc & Chantal Design	Hong Kong
www.me.com.hk/dmusic	Media Explorer Ltd.	Hong Kong
www.mitsubishicars.com.tw	米格多媒體股份有限公司	Taiwan
www.momojane.com	Kim Seeyeon	Korea
www.moove.com.au	Mementum Pty. Ltd.	Australia
www.mountup.com.au	Mark Bryant	Australia
www.neostream.com	Neostream Interactive	Australia
www.newpencil.com	Neostream Interactive	Australia
www.nexpo21.com	Kim Hae Jin	Korea
www.nike.com.hk	e-Crusade Marketing Co. Ltd.	Hong Kong
www.oblivia.com.au	The Attik	Australia
www.ohoneoh.com	O H	O N E	O H	China
www.onestudio.com	One Studio (HK) Ltd.	Hong Kong
www.onewomen.com	One Studio (HK) Ltd.	Hong Kong
www.ownflash.com	Chan Chi Chiu	China
www.pacificconnections.com	Pacific Connections Ltd.	Hong Kong
www.pacificplace.com.hk	Modem Media (HK) Limited	Hong Kong
palandri.chromeglobal.com	CHROME Global Company	Australia
www.panasonic-hk.com	Media Explorer Ltd	Hong Kong
www.parexcellence.com	The Web Connection	Hong Kong
www.pepsi.no	Mediafront As	Norway
www.photocity.co.kr	Nworks	Korea
www.planetpropaganda.com	Corey Szopinski	U.S.A.
playzone.acergame.com.tw/event/weblympics/	Acer Internet Services Inc.	Taiwan
puooet.getserver.com	朱甚月	China
www.purenz.com/saver1.cfm	Shift	New Zealand
www.quiksilver.com.au	Spin New Media	Australia
www.redant.com.au	Red Ant Design	Australia
www.reloade.com.au	Fredy D Ore	Australia
www.royalelastics.com	Urban Buffalo Creative	Australia
www.saintgeran.com	The Web Connection	Hong Kong
www.sanmiguel.com.hk	Media Explorer Ltd.	Hong Kong
www.sen-yeong.com	找思視覺媒體	Taiwan
services.sunday.com	Modem Media (HK) Limited	Hong Kong
www.silconcybertech.com	Silcon CyberTech Ltd.	Hong Kong
www.singapore.cnet.com	Asiacontent.com Media Pte. Ltd.	Singapore
www.singapore21.org.sg	Web Synergies (S) Pte. Ltd.	Singapore
www.smart-production.com	Lui Wing Ling	Hong Kong
www.solo.no	Mediafront As	Norway

URL	DESIGN	COUNTRY
www.spike.com	Spike CyberWorks	Australia
www.standardchartered.com	Beans Factory Hong Kong Co. Ltd.	Hong Kong
www.stareasy.com	Stareasy.com	Hong Kong
www.startechmm.com	Startech Multimedia Pte. Ltd.	Singapore
www.studioanybody.com/dean/memoriesrevisited.html	Dean Millson	Australia
www.subaru.com.au	Leo Burnett	Australia
www.sylvan.net	Gr8	U.S.A.
www.tendigital.com.au	Sausage Ltd.	Australia
www.the-emagination.com	e-magination.com	Singapore
www.toyota.com.au/avalon	Spike CyberWorks	Australia
www.toyota.com.au/celica	Spike CyberWorks	Australia
www.toyota.com.au/echo	Spike CyberWorks	Australia
www.toyota.com.au/mr2spyder	Saatchi & Saatchi	Australia
www.toyota.om.tw	Ogilvy Interactive	Taiwan
www.tradecentre.com.au	Justyn Walker	Australia
www.traveland.com.au	Massive Interactive Pty. Ltd.	Australia
www.trio.com.hk	Trio Interactive Co. Ltd.	Hong Kong
www.twofootedman.com/bluefish.html	twofootedman.com	U.S.A.
www.urban-buffalo.com	Urban Buffalo Creative	Australia
www.vdigm.com	Lee Dong Mi	Korea
www.vqmagazine.com	Tommy Li Design Workshop Ltd.	Hong Kong
www.wellcom.co.kr	Cho Keun Hae, Cho Keun Young	Korea
www.wys.com.cn/silkbook	iWorkshop China	China
www.xerts.com	Short Fuse Animation Pty. Ltd.	Australia
xm-folio.com/coca-cola/index.shtml	CCG.XM Pte. Ltd.	Singapore
xm-folio.com/compaq/ipaq/index.shtml	CCG.XM Pte. Ltd.	Singapore
xm-folio.com/compaq/presario800/index.shtml	CCG.XM Pte. Ltd.	Singapore
xm-folio.com/compaq/slimtower/index.shtml	CCG.XM Pte. Ltd.	Singapore
xm-folio.com/nokia/8850/demo/index.html	CCG.XM Pte. Ltd.	Singapore

// e-business

www.1024design.com	1024 Design	Australia
www.1stop-toys.com	1stop-toys.com	Hong Kong
www.2bsure.com	2bsure.com Pte. Ltd.	Malaysia
www.admango.com	Eureka Digital Limited	Hong Kong
www.adprocess.com	Adprocess	Hong Kong
www.adsociety.com	Lemon(Asia) Ltd.	Hong Kong
www.adworks.com	Gr8	U.S.A.
www.alexanderscigars.com.au	Creative Vision	Australia
www.arcotect.com/macromedia	Arcotect	Hong Kong

URL	DESIGN	COUNTRY
www.b2bcast.com	Mohana Khakhar	Singapore
www.b2system.com	Jung In Kwon	Korea
www.beansfactory.com	Eric Sun	Hong Kong
www.boags.com.au	Creative Vision	Australia
www.campaustralia.com.au	Square Circle Triangle Pty. Ltd.	Australia
www.creativateam.com	CreativaTEAM	Singapore
www.dchotomy.com	d:chotomy	Singapore
www.ddbi.com.hk/macromedia/charityglobal/content.htm	Tribal DDB Hong Kong	Hong Kong
design.javarer.com	J@Design Inc.	Hong Kong
www.diasham.com.sg	Kinetic Interactive Pte. Ltd.	Singapore
www.direction.net	An Young Hoon	Korea
www.discountnewcars.com.au	Creative Factory	Australia
www.enterprise.cwo.com.au	Leo Burnett	Australia
www.ewitewit.com	Ewit Co., Ltd.	Thailand
www.expoman.com	Beans Factory Hong Kong Co. Ltd.	Hong Kong
www.frekenbox.com	Sarunas Vaitkous	Australia
www.ga-media.com	Great Art Multi-Media Company	Hong Kong
www.gr8.com	Gr8	U.S.A.
www.handphoneas.co.kr	Park Young Min	Korea
www.hmit.co.kr	Park Jee Eun, Park Ji Young	Korea
home.hanmir.com/~pigu	Lim Myong Gu	Korea
www.i-sketch.com	i-sketch	Hong Kong
www.ifuni.com	Kim Che Yeon, Moon Hyung Jin	Korea
www.incube8.com	Gr8	U.S.A.
www.jardineschindler.com	Lemon (Asia) Ltd.	Hong Kong
www.jfax.com.au	Mediacom-IT	Australia
www.jobasia.com	Saiman Lee	Hong Kong
www.jongrottl.co.kr	Park Young Min	Korea
www.koreea.net	Lee Hyang Joo	Korea
www.kyungli.com	Kim Sae Yun	Korea
www.licence.71195.com	Gathering Design	Hong Kong
www.logicspace.com	Logicspace Limited	Hong Kong
www.matchlogic.com	Excite@Home	U.S.A.
www.media-genesis.com	Mohana Khakhar	Singapore
www.metamatrix.com	Gr8	U.S.A.
www.mljs.co.jp	Beans Factory Hong Kong Co. Ltd.	Hong Kong
www.mmedia.533.net	廣州日廣告公司	China
www.monashonline.com.au	Creative Factory	Australia
www.newtechmedia.com.au	Newtech Media Pty. Ltd.	Australia
www.northlinefreight.com.au	Redblue Design	Australia
www.ozanimation.com	Bun Heang Ung	Australia
www.pacim.com	Pacificlink iMedia Limited	Hong Kong

URL	DESIGN	COUNTRY
www.patties.com.au	Creative Vision	Australia
www.penfold.com.au	Square Circle Triangle P/L	Australia
www.pharmaz.net	Acmedia (S) Pte. Ltd.	Singapore
www.polycomasia.com	Mohana Khakhar	Singapore
www.pringles.com.cn	巡京華	China
www.quamnet.com	Quamnet.com	Hong Kong
www.red-eye.com.au	Creative Vision	Australia
www.roonets.com	Chung Sun Woo	Korea
www.seidler.net.au	Gary Venter	Australia
www.shaw.com.au	Redblue Design	Australia
www.shkp.com.hk	Saiman Lee	Hong Kong
skybusiness.com/ricamy/index99.html	Cheah Cheng Teik	Malaysia
www.softvill.com	Jang Seok Kyung	Korea
www.sourcenetworks.com.au	Leo Burnett	Australia
www.stickittome.co.nz	Turing Solutions (Ltd.)	New Zealand
www.streamingasia.com	Logicspace Limited	Hong Kong
www.sydneymediacollective.com.au/panasonic/update16/	Sydney Media Collective	Australia
www.sysweb.co.kr	Chun Jin Young	Korea
www.tab.co.nz	ZIVO New Zealand Limited	New Zealand
www.theatrearts-export.com	Nectarine	Australia
user.chollian.net/~mj96	Min Communications	Korea
www.vaneyk.com	Creative Factory	Australia
www.vodafone.net.nz	ZIVO New Zealand Limited	New Zealand
web.logicworld.com.au/~stevecox/	Steve Cox	Australia
www.web-works.com	Webworks Co. Ltd.	Thailand
www.weddingsave.co.kr	Kim Si Young	Korea
www.worldsites.net	Chun Byung Keun	Korea
www.woz.com.au/	Michael Worobec	Australia
www.xmlportal.co.kr	Lee Miyoung	Korea
www.youlim.co.kr	Kim Young Hwa	Korea

// e-commerce

www.01cyberlink.com	零壹媒體所	Hong Kong
www.21cdn.com	廣州日廣告公司	China
www.4376zone.com	Eureka Digital Limited	Hong Kong
www.77mm.com	77MM	Hong Kong
www.actionasia.com	One Studio (HK) Ltd.	Hong Kong
www.avoncity.co.nz	Warren McIntosh	New Zealand
www.bankcomm.com.hk	Pacificlink iMedia Ltd.	Hong Kong
www.banking.hsbc.com.hk	The Web Connection	Hong Kong
www.banyantravel.com	BanyanTreeWorld.com Pte. Ltd.	Singapore

URL	DESIGN	COUNTRY
www.bigfishmusic.com.au	Mal Huddleston	Australia
www.bridalbabe.com	Gr8	U.S.A.
www.cameraaction.com.au	Rik Evans-Deane	Australia
www.cathaypacific.com	The Web Connection	Hong Kong
www.citibank-icard.com	Modem Media (HK) Limited	Hong Kong
www.ckw-ibanking.com	Media Explorer Ltd.	Hong Kong
www.colinheaney.com/	Laura Harris	Australia
www.colorado.com.au	Zivo Pty. Ltd.	Australia
www.concavescream.com.sg	Kinetic Interactive Pte. Ltd.	Singapore
www.createevent.com/	Anirban Basu	India
www.creationstreet.com/	Latitude Web Pte. Ltd.	Singapore
www.cybersl.com	Modem Media (HK) Limited	Hong Kong
www.danofitness.com.hk	Gloria Lui Chung Yin	Hong Kong
www.ddbi.com.hk/macromedia/charityglobal/	Tribal DDB Hong Kong	Hong Kong
www.edgesolution.com	EdgeSolution(International) Ltd.	China
www.elfads.com	Pef Media, Inc.	U.S.A.
www.fincontrol.com	Glass Onion	Australia
www.gochinago.com	Lemon(Asia) Ltd.	Hong Kong
www.goophy.com	Mediafront As	Norway
www.gyroweb.cjb.net	GyroWeb	Australia
www.happyspender.com	Saiman Lee	Hong Kong
www.house18.com	InformAsia Holding Limited	Hong Kong
www.houseofyinyang.com	Pacificlink iMedia Ltd.	Hong Kong
www.i-lifeworld.com	Lemon(Asia) Ltd.	Hong Kong
www.i-voglia.com	Trio Interactive Co. Ltd.	Hong Kong
www.imdadcolors.com	Mohammed Imdad Vilah	India
www.innovision-net.com	Innovision Net Ltd.	Hong Kong
www.iteru.net	Kinetic Interactive Pte. Ltd.	Singapore
www.jamour.com	Comi Digital Ltd.	Hong Kong
www.jvc.com.hk	Lemon(Asia) Ltd.	Hong Kong
www.kulturhotel.at	Virtual DynamiX	Austria
www.legalstudio.com	Modem Media (HK) Limited	Hong Kong
www.lg.com.sg	Kinetic Interactive Pte. Ltd.	Singapore
www.metmuseum.org	Helene Germain	U.S.A.
www.mpfdirect.com	The Web Connection	Hong Kong
www.nxspace.com	Pandora Interactive Studio Pte. Ltd.	Singapore
www.orthodot.com.au	Morpheum	Australia
www.pegasus-fund.com	Pacificlink iMedia Ltd.	Hong Kong
www.pestbusters.com.sg	Kinetic Interactive Pte. Ltd.	Singapore
www.playadz.com	Kinetic Interactive Pte. Ltd.	Singapore
www.print12.com	iWorkshop China	China

URL	DESIGN	COUNTRY
www.print2sk.com	迅昌彩藝（深圳）有限公司	China
www.saa.org.hk	BEENET	Hong Kong
safedebit.qsipayments.com	QSI Payments	Australia
www.sandwichdirect.com	Danin Kahn	Australia
www.satanshirts.com	WebMedia	New Zealand
www.shangri-la.com	Modem Media (HK) Limited	Hong Kong
www.smart-livingplus.com	E-commerce Resources Limited	Hong Kong
www.spongestore.com	Citrus Internet	Australia
www.sunday.com	Lemon(Asia) Ltd.	Hong Kong
www.travelweb.com.sg	Acmedia (S) Pte. Ltd.	Singapore
www.webmedia.co.nz	WebMedia	New Zealand
www.wellplanet.com	Gr8	U.S.A.
www.yha.org.nz/	Turing Solutions (Ltd.)	New Zealand
www.yohifi.com	Halfkilo (HK) Limited	Hong Kong
www.zanyfun.com.au	Webmatchit Interactive Ltd.	Australia
zurich.com.sg	Web Synergies (S) Pte. Ltd.	Singapore

// lower education

www.alexphung.50megs.com	i-Venture (M) Sdn. Bhd.	Malaysia
www.anzacsite.gov.au	Mark Williams	Australia
apple.yesnew.com	重慶新人類	China
www.aviku.com	錢樾	China
www.bizarre07.com	So Won-young	Korea
www.civiad.com/sun757	廣東思域廣告有限公司	China
www.crankmedia.com.au/inhouse	Crank Media	Australia
www.crankmedia.com.au/thecircle	Crank Media	Australia
www.crankmedia.com.au/what	Crank Media	Australia
curriculum.edu.au/accessasia/goindonesia	Curriculum Corporation	Australia
www.easyscience.co.nz	Alan Knightbridge	New Zealand
www.edcreative.org	Tach Media Limited	Hong Kong
www.fahan.tas.edu.au/macquarie_island	Susan, Fflur, Williams, Higgs	Australia
www.geocities.com/takoi2000	Lau Ka-man (The HK Polytechnic University)	Hong Kong
www.gotafe.vic.edu.au	Goulburn Ovens Institute of TAFE	Australia
hkcee.oe21.com	Chateau Consultants Co. Ltd.	Hong Kong
home.pchome.com.tw/art/gw_monde	李涵棻	Taiwan
homex.coolconnect.com/member3/anne_ng/	Ng Ann Nee	Malaysia
www.ippyonline.gov.au/bounce/default.asp	Australia Government	Australia
www.iyellowbus.com	netalone.com Limited	Hong Kong
www.kidsedge.com	Knowledge Kids Network	U.S.A.
www.kidshealthandfitness.com.au	Deepend Sydney	Australia

// lower education

URL	DESIGN	COUNTRY
library.thinkquest.org/C001258	Simmon Chen	U.S.A.
www.ooliesputnik.com	Lai Boon Thye	Singapore
www.powerup.com.au/~dgillman/cyberrangers/	David Gillman	Australia
www.smcc.qld.edu.au	St. Mary's Catholic College	Australia
www.students.trinity.wa.edu.au/library	Trinity College	Australia
www.surf.to/dreameyes	Shirly Khaw	Malaysia
www.tahatai.school.nz/classes/room21/zerowastesite/homepage.html	Tahatai Coast School	New Zealand
www.tahatai.school.nz/classes/room24/index.html	Tahatai Coast School	New Zealand
www.tahatai.school.nz/classes/room7/virtualart.html	Tahatai Coast School	New Zealand
www.taylormade.co.nz/amanda/iread_cd_rom.zip	Scholastic Australia Pty. Ltd.	Australia
www.wetnwise.com	Show-Ads Interactive	Australia
www.whanganui.ac.nz/parents/	Dept Computer Graphics Whanganui Polytechnic	New Zealand
www.zanyfun.com.au	Webmatchit Interactive Ltd.	Australia

// higher education

URL	DESIGN	COUNTRY
158.132.218.202/~rachelchung/color/index.html	Daisy Chan (The HK Polytechnic University)	Hong Kong
166.111.107.2/digit-media/index.htm	劉惠芬	China
202.85.137.16:8900	Simple Multimedia Ltd.	Hong Kong
www.aiid.bee.qut.edu.au/ID/index.html	Philippe Vipathkun	Australia
www.ballarat.edu.au/arts/online	School of Arts, University of Ballarat	Australia
bravecity.eduweb.vic.gov.au	Rhythm Media Pty. Ltd.	Australia
www.britannica.com/reef	Massive Interactive Pty. Ltd.	Australia
www.bycomma.com/~hsnam	Nam Hyeop Soo	Korea
www.clubjd.co.kr	You Eun Kyung	Korea
www.coat.ke.ly	Agabang	Korea
www.ddbi.com.hk/macromedia/chinakids/content.htm	Tribal DDB Hong Kong	Hong Kong
dev.elc.polyu.edu.hk/wap/waponline/main.asp	The Hong Kong Polytechnic University	Hong Kong
www.dinayer.com/dinayer/index.html	Kim Taiyup	U.S.A.
www.eatart.net	Youn Ju-hee	Korea
www.englishone.com	Gr8	U.S.A.
www.eSchool-World.com	eSchool Limited	Hong Kong
www.eureka.pe.kr	Park Chan Min	Korea
www.exstudio.com	Moon Heung Jin	Korea
www.flashnara.com	Park Sung Hwan	Korea
folkart.at.china.com	袁袋紘	China
www.galaxygoo.com	Kristin Henry	U.S.A.
www.hkbu.edu.hk	Cheung Wai Hung	Hong Kong
home.hanmir.com/~yousw	You Seung Won	Korea
home.pchome.com.tw/computer/box715/	張文蓓	Taiwan
home.ust.hk/~im_lwxaa/cufinearts/index.htm	Ko Siu Hong	Hong Kong

URL	DESIGN	COUNTRY
hoony.kbsart.co.kr	Song Hoon	Korea
www.jmi.co.kr	Jung Yeom	Korea
www.jumptoart.com	Wong Chung Yu	Hong Kong
www.kebi.com/~cocobox	Shin So Young	Korea
kiony.pe.ky	Kim Young Min	Korea
www.kkk.pr.kr	Kim Hyun Gum	Korea
www.lassomedia.com	Yoo Hye Jong	Canada
lhk1130.hihome.com	Lee Hee Kyung	Korea
www.linemass.com	Choi Woo Yeon	Korea
members.tripod.co.kr/~boozzi	Kim Eun Mi	Korea
members.tripod.co.kr/~hwanginyoung	Hwang In Young	Korea
members.tripod.lycos.co.kr/coboy/	Sung Yong Jin	Korea
members.tripod.lycos.co.kr/lsm32	Lee Sang Mi	Korea
members.tripod.lycos.co.kr/webi	Choi Yong Jin	Korea
www.meowism.com	微妙軟體	Taiwan
mup.yuntech.edu.tw	共正雄	Taiwan
my.dreamwiz.com/a2528	Yeon Kyung Ah	Korea
my.netian.com/~ninog	Noh In kyung	Korea
myhome.dreamx.net/d010b	Ok Sae Hoon	Korea
myhome.hananet.net/~sicily	Lee Byung Wook	Korea
myhome.hananet.net/~tears4me	Lee Chooyoul	Korea
myhome.shinbiro.com/ckb72	Choi Ki Bae	Korea
myhome.thrunet.com/~aimhigh	Kim Sung Hyuk	Korea
mypage.channeli.net/~sun2063	Kim Sun Young	Korea
www.newcastle.edu.au/uniunion/cyber/cycle.htm	Paul Harrison	Australia
www.nyp.edu.sg/sit/fusion2000	Isabelle Tan	Singapore
www.nyp.edu.sg/sit/intro.html	Xin Mei Yu	Singapore
www.nyp.edu.sg/sit/routemap/index.html	Eric Eng	Singapore
olt.qut.edu.au/temp/beams/	Talss Smile (Queensland University of Technology)	Australia
www.online.swin.edu.au/lts/ed_dev/flexhtm	Swinburne University of Technology	Australia
www.online.swin.edu.au/wwwhat/questions/	Swinburne University of Technology	Australia
www.ozemail.com.au/~beilharz	Kirsty Beilharz	Australia
www.phm.gov.au/ancient_greek_olympics/	Massive Interactive Pty. Ltd.	Australia
www.science-architecture.com	Gianluca Milesi	U.S.A.
www.seoleuna.com	Seol Eun-A	Korea
www.somaa.intizen.com	Chun Hyun Kyung	Korea
www.sylvanatschool.com	Gr8	U.S.A.
www.taiyup.com	Kim Taiyup	Korea
www.twenty4.com.au	Twenty4 - Design & Communication	Australia
www.unisanet.unisa.edu.au/07031/macro_frame.html	University of South Australia	Australia
www.unitec.ac.nz	UNITEC	New Zealand

// higher education

URL	DESIGN	COUNTRY
unju33.hihome.com	Jang Un Ju	Korea
www.wallstreetinstitute.com	Gr8	U.S.A.
www.yoonsun.com	Joo Yoonsun	Korea
zzagn.net/ani95	Kim So Young	Korea
zzagn.net/eunyang	Kim Eun Yang	Korea

// entertainment

URL	DESIGN	COUNTRY
www.17play.com.sg	Asiacontent.com Media Pte. Ltd.	Singapore
www.3words.com	Dayo Sowunmi	Australia
www.72ppi.com	Matthew Willis	Australia
www.8arts.com	Asiacontent.com Media Pte. Ltd.	Singapore
www.acergame.com.tw	Acer Internet Services Inc.	Taiwan
www.acmabooks.com	acmabooks.com Pte. Ltd.	Singapore
www.acmabooks.com/books/chapter/chapter.html	Patrick Chua	Singapore
www.againsthegrain.com	Against The Grain Sdn. Bhd.	Malaysia
www.alcohol.org.nz/fuel/game.html	Shift	New Zealand
www.alvr1.com	Joseph Lee	Philippines
www.antinow.com	曾權輝	Hong Kong
www.art-bugs.com	Pong Phui Hin	Malaysia
asia.eonline.com	Asiacontent.com Media Pte. Ltd.	Singapore
www.atomicattack.com	Calvin Ho	Hong Kong
www.bitlounge.com	Joshua Lim	Malaysia
www.brittle-bones.com	Marc Stricklin	U.S.A.
www.cafe-infinity.com	Adam & Luke Heise	Australia
www.cartoonnetwork.com.au	Meredith Coleman	Australia
www.cartoonplaza.net	Kim Jong Eun	Korea
www.cestlav.com	Star TV (Channel V)	Hong Kong
www.chi-key.com	Dominic Sinclair Goldman	Singapore
www.click2music.co.kr	Comma Communication	Korea
www.cocacola.com.au	Spin New Media	Australia
www.cokebuddy.com.au	Spin New Media	Australia
www.colorsmagazine.com	Steve Lawler	Italy
www.comicinema.com	Comi Infinet Technology Ltd.	Hong Kong
www.cosmstudio.com	Justin Lin	Taiwan
www.dartweb.com.au	Mark Bryant	Australia
www-des.tp.edu.sg/course/d4internet2/project/sk8/index0.htm	Leung Pui San	Singapore
www-des.tp.edu.sg/course/d4internet2/project/freshid/html/splash.htm	Jeannie Neo Yong Ling	Singapore
www-des.tp.edu.sg/students/candice_koh/party.html	Candice Koh Yun-Jia	Singapore
www-des.tp.edu.sg/students/lee_ros/index.htm	Ros Lee Shook Kwen	Singapore
www-des.tp.edu.sg/students/lim_hui_ling/index.html	Lim Hui Ling	Singapore
www-des.tp.edu.sg/students/Tan_Wee_Thong/index.htm	Tan Wee Thong	Singapore

URL	DESIGN	COUNTRY
www.doldo.com	Same Dream	China
www.edenstudio.com/portfolio/taibeer/openning.htm	Eden Studio	Taiwan
www.ericsoart.com	Eric So	Hong Kong
www.exspace.com	Acmedia (S) Pte. Ltd.	Singapore
www.eyeost.com	Baek Myung Ki	Korea
www.faye.com	Irene Santoso	U.S.A.
www.foxmovies.com.au	Massive Interactive Pty. Ltd.	Australia
www.freedrum.com	Andrew Garton	Australia
www.geocities.com/dreamland2010/flash/duck.html	Peng Lu	Singapore
www.geocities.com/jimjacke	Chow Lai Ching	Hong Kong
www.geocities.com/pohlingz	Khoo Poh Ling	Singapore
www.geocities.com/wwwhat_1/cammy/index.htm	Tang Hiu Wan (Hong Kong Institute of Vocational Education)	Hong Kong
www.geocities.com/wwwhat_1/catherine/index.htm	Leung Po Chui (Hong Kong Institute of Vocational Education)	Hong Kong
www.geocities.com/wwwhat_2/lucia/final.html	Ho Tan Hung (Hong Kong Institute of Vocational Education)	Hong Kong
www.geocities.com/wwwhat_2/paul/FINAL.HTML	Paul Yip (Hong Kong Institute of Vocational Education)	Hong Kong
www.geocities.com/wwwhat_2/scott/Begin.html	Yankit Wong (Hong Kong Institute of Vocational Education)	Hong Kong
www.geocities.com/wwwhat_2/yau/Deda.html	Yau Tai Hing (Hong Kong Institute of Vocational Education)	Hong Kong
www.geocities.com/wwwhat_3/katie/WebFinal.html	Ho Tan Hung (Hong Kong Institute of Vocational Education)	Hong Kong
www.geocities.com/wwwhat_3/lucia/final.html	Ho Tan Hung (Hong Kong Institute of Vocational Education)	Hong Kong
www.geocities.com/wwwhat_3/sam/index1.html	Sam Ching Win Sze (Hong Kong Institute of Vocational Education)	Hong Kong
www.geocities.com/wwwhat_3/yau/Work.swf	Yau Tai Hing (Hong Kong Institute of Vocational Education)	Hong Kong
www.geocities.com/wwwhat_4/chan/index.html	Chan Ho (Hong Kong Institute of Vocational Education)	Hong Kong
www.geocities.com/wwwhat_4/cheng/finalfinal2copy.html	Chen Shek Ming (Hong Kong Institute of Vocational Education)	Hong Kong
www.geocities.com/wwwhat_4/dave/BOXXX.html	Choi Kai Fung (Hong Kong Institute of Vocational Education)	Hong Kong
www.geocities.com/wwwhat_4/html/web_fin.htm	Fung Ming Lok (Hong Kong Institute of Vocational Education)	Hong Kong
www.geocities.com/wwwhat_4/kwok/set.htm	Kwok Yat-Lam (Hong Kong Institute of Vocational Education)	Hong Kong
www.geocities.com/wwwhat_4/law/PLAYST1.SWF	Law Man-chung (Hong Kong Institute of Vocational Education)	Hong Kong
www.geocities.com/wwwhat_4/olivia/faye.html	Olivia Chan (Hong Kong Institute of Vocational Education)	Hong Kong
www.geocities.com/wwwhat_4/orli/Chows.html	Orli Chow (Hong Kong Institute of Vocational Education)	Hong Kong
www.geocities.com/wwwhat_5/happy/cell.html	Fai Yu (Hong Kong Institute of Vocational Education)	Hong Kong

URL	DESIGN	COUNTRY
www.geocities.com/wwwhat_5/maureen/opennning.html	Maureen Mak Mei Lin (Hong Kong Institute of Vocational Education)	Hong Kong
www.geocities.com/wwwhat_6/sam/index.html	Sam Ching Win Sze (Hong Kong Institute of Vocational Education)	Hong Kong
www.geocities.com/WWWhat_7/tony/index.html	So Chi Ming (Hong Kong Institute of Vocational Education)	Hong Kong
www.girlno1.com.tw	春暉國際多媒體	Taiwan
go.to/eoc	Siu Chin To (Hong Kong Institute of Vocational Education)	Hong Kong
goto.fashionguide.net/opsite	楊家俊	Taiwan
www.harriman-leasing.com	Brian Loh	Hong Kong
home.i-cable.com/fatching	Ching Ching (Hong Kong Institute of Vocational Education)	Hong Kong
home.kcnet5.com/~cyberweb	Choi Kun-ho	Korea
www.humpbackoak.com	Sean Lam	Singapore
i7sport.i7.com.au	Sausage Ltd.	Australia
www.icon-nicholson.com/holiday99	Icon Nicholson	U.S.A.
www.inhalex.com	Delapse Broadcast Design and Animation	South Africa
www.jmi.co.kr	Lee Hyun Joo	Korea
www.joeworld.net	Pandora Interactive Studio Pte. Ltd.	Singapore
www.jollyzone.com	Pacificlink iMedia Ltd.	Hong Kong
www.juice.com.tw	和信超媒體	Taiwan
kink.hk.st	Lau Chi Kin	Hong Kong
www.krening.com	Karen Ingram	U.S.A.
kubrick.cdes.qut.edu.au/~n2534339/aab626/index.html	Jane Ellery	Australia
www.kungfuboy.com	Davidcan.com Pte. Ltd.	Singapore
lesliezhu.myrice.com	Leslie Chu Wui Wing	Hong Kong
www.l-o-u-d-3d.com	L-O-U-D	Australia
www.managingtheplanet.com	Denise Tai	Malaysia
www.mars.idv.tw	Mars Huang	Taiwan
www.meanone.com	DNA Studio	U.S.A.
www.mebag.com	國立台灣藝術學院	Taiwan
members.tripod.com/~qinkey	Andrew Tan	Singapore
members.xoom.com/_XMCM/penism/htm/main.htm	Au Chun Leong (Hong Kong Institute of Vocational Education)	Hong Kong
www.mezzatype.com	Patric Chua	Singapore
www.molvaermusic.com	Mediafront As	Norway
www.mtv.com/mtv/marketing/zippo/paint18.jhtml	Tree-Axis	U.S.A.
www.mtv.com/sendme.tin?page=/mtv/tubescan/roadrules/marketing/game/index.html	Tree-Axis	U.S.A.
www.mtv2.co.uk	Digit	UK
www.music4nothing.com	Mohana Khakhar	Singapore
www.musicbox.co.kr	No Jae Kyung	Korea
myhome.hananet.net/~sicily	Lee Byung Kook	Korea
www.mysteryclock.com	Mystery Clock Cinema	Australia

URL	DESIGN	COUNTRY
www.neopod.net/thepixelpeople/	Liam Wolf	Australia
www.neroliwesley.com.au/baggage/	Neroli Wesley	Australia
www.netfun.com	Net Fun Limited	Hong Kong
www.netshelter.net	Michael Worobec	Australia
www.nurse-betty.com	DNA Studio	U.S.A.
www.oi.co.kr	Cho Hyun Joo	Korea
www.operanuda.com	Operanuda	Netherlands
www.optusgame.wce.com.au:84/default.asp?userteam=1	Leo Burnett	Australia
www.oreo.com.tw	Eden Studio	Taiwan
www.oval-design.com	Eddie Cheung Chi Chung (Hong Kong Institute of Vocational Education)	Hong Kong
www.OzDreamTime.com.au	Kirsty Beilharz	Australia
www.partyharder.com	MCM Entertainment Online	Australia
www.planetmg.com	Latitude Web Pte. Ltd.	Singapore
playzone.acergame.com.tw	Acer Internet Services Inc.	Taiwan
playzone.acergame.com.tw/event/weblympics/	Acer Internet Services Inc.	Taiwan
playzone.acergame.com.tw/ghostzone/index.html	Acer Internet Services Inc.	Taiwan
www.p-o-e.com	DNA Studio	U.S.A.
www.postkard.com	Postlard.com	China
www.projectbox.com	Krisakorn Tantitemit	Thailand
www.saulbass.co.uk/psychostudio/	Brendan Dawes	UK
www.shanghainoon.com.au	Spin New Media	Australia
site.fdnet.com.au/flashman/	Susan Flashman	Australia
www.spe.sony.com/movies/charliesangels	DNA Studio	U.S.A.
www.spe.sony.com/movies/hollowman	DNA Studio	U.S.A.
www.spe.sony.com/movies/verticallimit	DNA Studio	U.S.A.
www.stickyplanet.com.au/key.swf	David Cassel	Australia
www.supastar.channelv.com.au	Walmac/Euro RSCG Interaction	Australia
www.suture.net	Ricky Cox	Australia
www.suwonlife.co.kr/internet.htm	Lee Joon Kyung	Korea
www.swatiwebdesign.com/temple/temples_of_india.htm	Swati Sanghani	India
www.take40.com	MCM Entertainment Online	Australia
www.Terminal2064.com	Ho Lai Lai	Hong Kong
www.theaudiosphere.com	Art Narara Pty. Ltd.	Australia
www.timecode2000.com	DNA Studio	U.S.A.
www.transience.com.au	Dave Jones	Australia
www.twofootedman.com/streetcrosser.html	twofootedman.com	U.S.A.
www.vraustralia.com	Daniel Box	Australia
www.webagent007.com	James Begera	U.S.A.
weiju.go.163.com	任娜為	China
www.wotch.com	Wotch.com	Australia
www.xcreate.com	XCREATE Company Limited	Hong Kong

// corporate training

URL	DESIGN	COUNTRY
xm-folio.com/coca-cola/ice_fishing_splash.shtml	CCG.XM Pte. Ltd.	Singapore
xm-folio.com/coca-cola/polar_bar_splash.shtml	CCG.XM Pte. Ltd.	Singapore
xm-folio.com/coca-cola/ski_challenge_splash.shtml	CCG.XM Pte. Ltd.	Singapore
xm-folio.com/coca-cola/writers_blok_splash.shtml	CCG.XM Pte. Ltd.	Singapore
xm-folio.com/coca-cola/xmas_cards_splash.shtml	CCG.XM Pte. Ltd.	Singapore
xm-folio.com/compaq/christmasgame99/index.html	CCG.XM Pte. Ltd.	Singapore
xm-folio.com/nokia/8210/8210_demo.shtml	CCG.XM Pte. Ltd.	Singapore
www.yayaya.cc	Cheung Wai Hung	Hong Kong
yesuede.yeah.net	詩敏	China
www.yippeeland.com	Yetisoft Limited	Hong Kong
www.zanyfun.com.au	Webmatchit Interactive Ltd.	Australia
163.23.33.230/mbase/learning/vod.html	大安大學	Taiwan
www.asiacontent.com	Asiacontent.com Media Pte. Ltd.	Singapore
www.ddbi.com.hk/macromedia/cisco/	Tribal DDB Hong Kong	Hong Kong
www.et21.com	Nanum Info-Tech	Korea
www.feelwith.co.kr	Cho Sung Bok	Korea
www.geocities.com/smiling_jin/hangul	Kang Hyunjin	Korea
home.hanmir.com/~pogo1	Lee Tae Woo	Korea
homepage.renren.com/dave	Dow Technologies	Hong Kong
www.imperialacademy.org	Jesse Boyce	Australia
www.knnbccb.com	Tang Howe Choon	Singapore
www.looktest.net	Choi Seung Il	Korea
www.soh.nsw.gov.au/files/calendar/kids/kids.html	Fizzy Cactus	Australia
www.sp9004.or.kr	Park Ji Young	Korea
www.y-english.com	Kim Nam Hyung	Korea

// government

URL	DESIGN	COUNTRY
www.burkeandwills.net	State Library of Victoria	Australia
www.charlessturt.sa.gov.au	Darren Falkenberg	Australia
www.class2u.com	王自正	Taiwan
www.cywi.co.kr/ccpost	Woo Nam Chul	Korea
www.gamesinfo.com.au/tripplanner/	Massive Interactive Pty. Ltd.	Australia
www.hkairport.com	Asia online (H.K.) Ltd.	Hong Kong
www.slv.vic.gov.au/slv/exhibitions/diaries/	State Library of Victoria	Australia
www.slv.vic.gov.au/slv/exhibitions/olympics/	State Library of Victoria	Australia
www.visitnsw.com.au	Leo Burnett	Australia

** Please note : the sites listed in the index contains only those which are still existing.